Happy Trails

A Pictorial Celebration of the Life and Times of
Roy Rogers *and* Dale Evans

HOWARD KAZANJIAN AND CHRIS ENSS

TWODOT®

GUILFORD, CONNECTICUT
HELENA, MONTANA
AN IMPRINT OF THE GLOBE PEQUOT PRESS

A · TWODOT® · BOOK

Copyright © 2005 by Chris Enss and Howard Kazanjian

TwoDot is a registered trademark of Morris Book Publishing, LLC.

Photographs courtesy of the Roy Rogers–Dale Evans family and museum
Spot images courtesy of Photos.com, Jan Cronan, Melissa Evarts, and Casey Shain
Book and jacket design by Casey Shain

Library of Congress Cataloging-in-Publication Data
Kazanjian, Howard.
    Happy trails: a pictorial celebration of the life and times of Roy Rogers and Dale Evans /
  Howard Kazanjian and Chris Enss.—1st ed.
        p. cm.
    Includes filmographies.
    Includes bibliographical references and index.
    ISBN 978-0-7627-3089-6
        1. Rogers, Roy, 1911- 2. Rogers, Dale Evans. 3. Rogers, Roy, 1911—Pictorial works.
4. Rogers, Dale Evans—Pictorial works. 5. Actors—United States—Biography.
6. Actors—United States—Pictorial works. 7. Singers—United States—Biography.
8. Singers—United States—Pictorial works. I. Enss, Chris, 1961- II. Title.
PN2287.R73K43 2004
791.4302'8'092—dc22
[B]
                                                                                    2004052326

Printed in China
First Edition/Second Printing

Contents

A Roy Rogers fan stands beside an advertisement of his hero.

Introduction

Hundreds of excited children, with hard-earned nickels and dimes clutched tightly in their fists, exchanged their money for a ticket at Saturday matinees across the country in the 1940s. The chance to see singing cowboy Roy Rogers, his horse, Trigger, and leading lady Dale Evans come up against the West's most notorious criminals brought young audiences to theaters in droves. And, in the process, it elevated western musicals to one of the most popular film genres in history.

Roy Rogers and Dale Evans were the reigning royalty of B-rated westerns for more than a decade. They helped persuade moviegoers that good always triumphs over evil in a fair fight and that life on the open range was one long, wholesome sing-along. Together, the King of the Cowboys and the Queen of the West appeared in more than 200 films and television programs.

Roy and Dale made their first picture together in 1944. The film, *The Cowboy and the Senorita,* brought an estimated 900,000 fans to movie houses in America and began a partnership for the couple that lasted fifty-two years. The

chemistry between Roy and Dale was enchanting, and together they were an entertainment powerhouse. In addition to their films, they had popular radio programs, comic book series, albums, and a long list of merchandise (including clothes, boots, and toys), all bearing their names.

Roy and Dale were successful individually, as well. Dale, a talented singer-songwriter, performed with big band orchestras, shared the stage with Edgar Bergen and Charlie McCarthy, and penned many popular tunes, including the song that would be Roy and Dale's theme, "Happy Trails." Roy was a co-founder and member of the group the Sons of the Pioneers. The band made a name for itself singing original country music songs, including "Cool Water" and "Tumblin' Tumbleweeds."

Roy Rogers and Dale Evans were married in 1947. As a couple they were consistently ranked in the top ten among the western stars at the box office.

The Cowboy and the Senorita *in 1944 was the first of twenty-nine motion pictures Roy Rogers and Dale Evans made together.*

They costarred in twenty-nine movies and recorded more than 200 albums together. In 1951, they parlayed their fame to the small screen, appearing in a half-hour television show aptly called *The Roy Rogers Show*.

When they weren't working, the western icons spent a great deal of time visiting children in hospitals and orphanages. They were dedicated Christians who sought to serve the hurt and needy. They would later be recognized by national civic organizations for their humanitarian efforts.

Roy and Dale pose for a publicity photo for the movie Don't Fence Me In.

Unaware, the first of her more than twenty books.

After the couple was semiretired from the entertainment industry, they greeted fans at their museum in Victorville, California, and enjoyed life with their children, grandchildren, and great-grandchildren. Thousands of western enthusiasts and fans alike now make the pilgrimage to Branson, Missouri, where the Roy Rogers–Dale Evans Museum is currently located. They come to get a glimpse of their heroes' six-shooters, boots, costumes, and other personal artifacts on display.

Roy and Dale's off-screen life was filled with a great deal of love and happiness. They had nine children, whom they adored and showered with affection. Their family was no stranger to tragedy, though. One child, Robin, died of complications associated with Down syndrome. An adopted daughter, Debbie, died in a church bus accident when she was twelve; their adopted son, Sandy, suffered an accidental death while serving in the military in Germany. Robin's death inspired Dale to write *Angel*

The Rogers family's collection of priceless items elicits fond memories of an inspirational pair who used their immense talent to encourage moral and spiritual strength. The artifacts draw visitors back in time to when knights of the American plains yodeled, wore white hats and fancy boots, and thrived on defeating the outlaws and rescuing the defenseless.

Chapter One

From Farmer to Actor

"They love this cowboy and his simple story full of vim and life, right and might. A story of a man's struggle with nature, of songs under the stars, and of a life as it should be lived."

Entertainment columnist Louella Parsons, explaining why audiences returned again and again to see Roy Rogers's movies—1938

Roy was just twenty-six
when he landed his first
movie contract.

Leonard was a natural with animals, nursing

puppies, pigs, and ponies back to health when

they got sick or had broken bones.

oy Rogers was born Leonard Franklin Slye on November 5, 1911, in Cincinnati, Ohio. His parents owned a farm near the small town of Duck Run, and it was there that he developed his love for music. By the age of ten he was playing the guitar and calling square dances.

In 1929 Leonard left the Midwest and headed for Hollywood. In between occasional singing engagements with the various bands he helped form (including the Sons of the Pioneers), he worked as a truck driver and a fruit picker.

His big break came in 1937, when he snuck onto the lot of Republic Pictures and landed a contract paying seventy-five dollars a week. Republic Studios' president Herbert Yates was looking for a musical actor to go boot-to-boot with singing-cowboy sensation Gene Autry. Renamed Roy Rogers, Leonard had the integrity, the talent, and the look the studio was hoping to find.

Three short years after signing with Republic, Roy Rogers would be the number-one box-office draw in the country and be crowned the King of the Cowboys.

Leonard (left) played at many "one-night-only" performances early in his career.

Farley's "Gold Star" Rangers

Leonard (right) performed as a member of Farley's Gold Star Rangers. In the early 1930s

he was also part of the Slye Brothers, The Rocky Mountaineers,

and the International Cowboys.

Mattie Slye's only son frequently credited his parents and three sisters as the musical influences in his life.

Chapter Two

From Secretary to Singer

"With her beautiful voice, good looks, and radiant personality, it was a foregone conclusion motion picture executives would put Dale Evans under contract."

Entertainment columnist Louella Parsons—1944

Dale Evans hoped her Republic Studios contract would eventually lead her to Broadway.

Frances and her brother, Hillman, take a ride on a donkey at their grandfather's ranch in Texas.

Dale Evans was born Frances Octavia Smith on October 31, 1912, in Uvalde, Texas. In her words, her upbringing was "idyllic." As the only daughter of Walter and Betty Sue Smith, she was showered with attention and her musical talents were encouraged with piano and dance lessons.

While still in high school, she married Thomas Fox and had a son, Thomas Jr. The marriage, however, was short-lived. After securing a divorce, she attended a business school in Memphis and worked as a secretary before making her singing debut at a local radio station. In 1931 she changed her name to Dale Evans.

By the mid 1930s, Dale was a highly sought-after big-band singer performing with orchestras throughout the Midwest. Her stage persona and singing voice earned her a screen test for the 1942 movie *Holiday Inn*. She didn't get the part, but she ended up signing with the nationally broadcast radio program the *Chase and Sanborn Hour* and soon after signed a contract with Republic Studios. She hoped her work in motion pictures would lead to a run on Broadway doing musicals.

A teenage Frances
gets ready to perform in
a dance recital in 1926.

At agent Joe Rivkin's request,

this early publicity photo of Dale

was sent to Hollywood.

This 1938 publicity photo of Dale was taken shortly after she signed a contract with Twentieth Century Fox.

Chapter Three

Republic's Cowboy

"I don't know what it is, but something draws you close to Roy Rogers. It may be his sincerity of purpose, his loyalty, his friendliness, or his good naturedness. It may be all of those things."

Roy's high school teacher Guy Baumgarner — Portsmouth (Ohio) Times, *August 1959*

Leonard joins other members of the Sons of the Pioneers on the set of a Republic Pictures western.

Leonard and fellow band members (shown in a 1936 photo) not only supplied music for westerns at Republic, but for Columbia Studios as well.

Before he got his big break, Leonard Slye toured the country with various bands he helped form. One such band, the Sons of the Pioneers, became a popular western group on Los Angeles radio station KFWB. By 1935 the five-member combo was playing a variety of dates and doing background music for motion pictures.

After hearing about a Republic casting call to find a new singing cowboy, Leonard decided to venture away from the troupe to audition. He snuck onto the studio lot and wound up in the office of the producer who had initiated the search for a singing cowboy. Leonard was just what the producer was looking for, and on October 13, 1937, a newly named Roy Rogers signed a contract with the studio.

Leonard entertains listeners at a radio performance in 1935.

Leonard serenades a studio audience during a radio show.

17

Roy poses for a Republic publicity shot in 1938.

Chapter Four

Singer, Dancer, Wife, and Mother

"She's a talented vocalist with a commanding stage presence. In my estimation she's one of the best entertainers around. Whether she's acting, dancing, or singing, or doing all three at once . . . it's a treat to watch her work."

Dale Evans fan Geoffery Hardgrove—Movie World Magazine, *1949*

Republic Studios used this publicity photo of Dale to promote the movies Here Comes Elmer *and* Hoosier Holiday.

Dale strikes a pose for her role in the 1943 Republic film
Swing Your Partner.

In August 1943, two weeks after signing a one-year contract with Republic Studios, Dale began rehearsals for the film *Swing Your Partner.* Although her role in the picture was small, studio executives considered it a promising start. Over the next year Dale filmed nine other movies for Republic, and in between she continued to record music.

When she wasn't working, Dale spent time with her son, Tom, and her second husband, orchestra director Robert Butts. Her marriage was struggling under the weight of their demanding work schedules, but neither spouse was willing to compromise.

"I was torn between my desire to be a good housekeeper, wife, and mother and my consuming ambition as an entertainer," Dale told the *Los Angeles Daily News* in 1970. "It was like trying to ride two horses at once, and I couldn't seem to control either one of them."

Dale's marriage might have been suffering, but her career was taking off. Republic Studios' president Herbert Yates summoned Dale to a meeting to discuss the next musical the studio would be doing. She took this as a hopeful sign. It was common knowledge around the studio lot that Yates had recently seen a New York stage production of the musical *Oklahoma* and had fallen in love with the story. Dale imagined that the studio president wanted to talk with her about starring in a film version of the play. It was the opportunity she had always envisioned for herself. For a brief moment she was one step closer to Broadway.

Dale poses for a
1941 glamour shot.

Chapter Five

Playboy of the Western World

"He was . . . the most genuine, down-to-earth person I've ever had the pleasure of knowing. Being associated with Roy and his family over the years has been the richest experience I could ever hope for."

Art Rush about his client Roy Rogers—1977

Roy takes a moment to enjoy the success from his first starring role in the 1938 Republic feature Under Western Stars.

Dallas politicians present Roy with a key to the city in 1938 after his first picture, Under Western Stars, *premiered there.*

Roy Rogers's first starring role came in the picture *Under Western Stars*. The film premiered in Dallas, Texas, in April 1938 and ushered in a new trend in westerns. In the process it rocketed the singing cowboy to stardom. Audiences made *Under Western Stars* a box office success and critics called its star "the new Playboy of the Western World."

Among Roy's biggest fans were his mother, Mattie, and father, Andrew. The pair followed their son's hit picture from theater to theater. Years later Roy had the studio make a personal print of the movie for his parents.

Fans all over the country sent letters to Roy Rogers. Roy and his wife, Arline, whom he married in 1936, sorted through the mail and answered each letter personally, paying for the postage themselves. Republic executives refused to pay for such a thing. Roy was adamant about responding to everyone who took the time to write to him, but as the letters piled up he realized he couldn't do the job alone. He eventually hired two secretaries to help him with the 20,000 pieces of fan mail he got each week.

Roy made thirty-six pictures for Republic between 1938 and 1942. His manager and best friend, Art Rush, not only handled his film career, but also arranged for his client to be the star of a radio serial titled *Manhattan Cowboy*. In addition, Art scheduled personal appearances for Roy at rodeos and parades. Both Roy's fame and his salary increased under Art's guidance. Republic was paying the singing cowboy a mere $75 a week, but the radio program and personal appearances earned him ten times that amount.

Roy received thousands of fan letters a week. He believed his fan letters should all be answered.

"If folks are nice enough to write to you, the only polite thing to do is answer."

Roy and the Sons of the Pioneers entertain the public on the road in 1941.

Trigger starred in eighty films with Roy and received more than 200 fan letters a month. Billboards announcing Roy's pictures were commonplace when the Cowboy was King.

Roy participated in hundreds of public appearances, including this one in 1944.

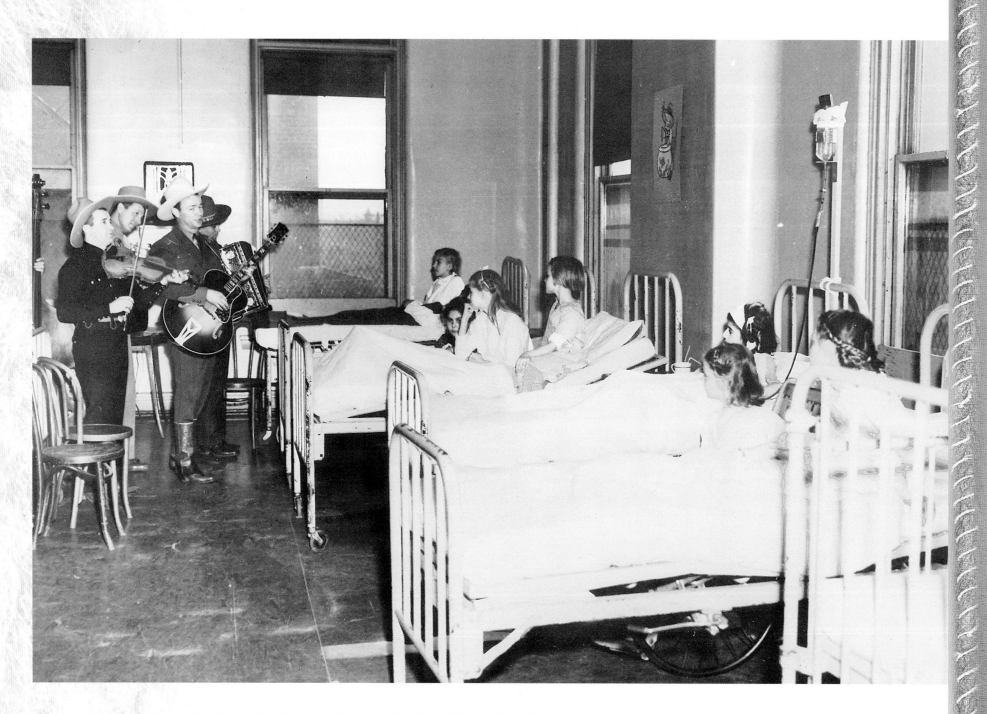

No matter how busy he was, Roy always took time to visit sick and hurting children in hospitals.

Roy Rogers and Gabby Hayes teamed up with leading lady Sally March in the 1939 film The Arizona Kid.

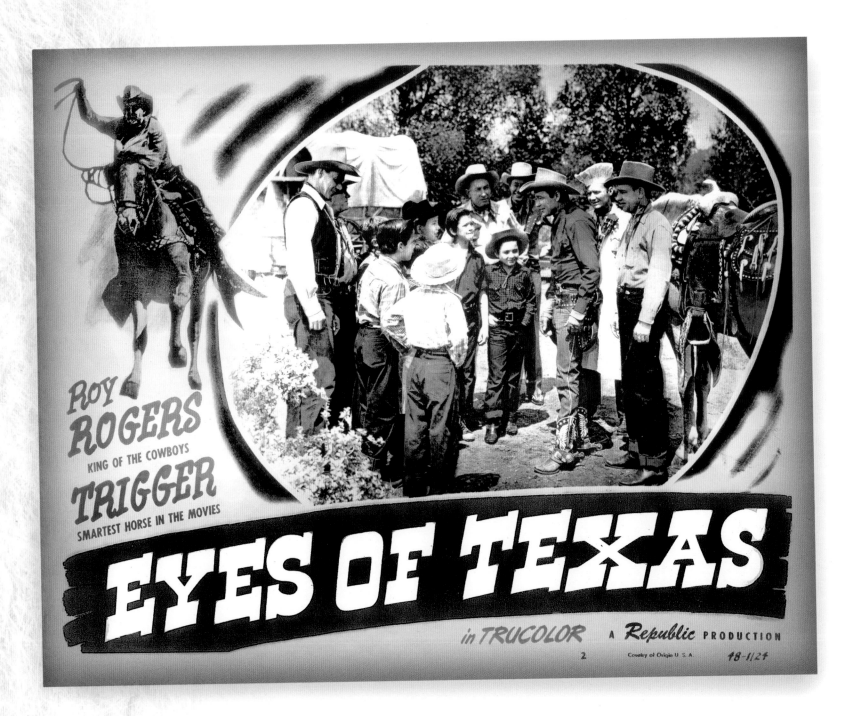

The 1948 film Eyes of Texas *featured Roy Rogers, Andy Devine, and Nana Bryant.*

Chapter Six

Leading Lady

"Dale embodied the credo of the West."

Actress Katharine Ross

A 1949 Republic Pictures promotional packet on B-western sensations Roy Rogers and Dale Evans included this photo.

Dale poses for a fashion spread for a movie magazine in 1942.

Dale Evans dreamed of starring as the lead in the film version of *Oklahoma,* but Republic president Herbert Yates had other plans for the actress. He wanted her to play opposite the studio's star cowboy in the movie *The Cowboy and the Senorita.*

Dale's only experience in westerns had been a small role as a saloon singer in a John Wayne picture, and she was not a skilled rider. She committed herself to doing her very best, however, in the role of the "Senorita," Ysobel Martinez.

The picture was released in 1944 and was a huge success. Theater managers and audiences alike encouraged studio executives at Republic to quickly re-team Dale and Roy in another western.

In between her film jobs, Dale toured military bases in the United States with the USO. She sang to troops on bivouac, from Louisiana to Texas. She was proud to think she was bringing a little sunshine into the hearts of the soldiers.

Dale also brought sunshine into the hearts of moviegoers, and ticket sales were evidence of that. Republic had happened onto the perfect western team. Dale was a sassy, sophisticated leading lady and the perfect foil for Roy, the patient, singing cowboy.

Dale gave many USO performances at military bases around the country in the 1940s.

A publicity photo shows the life of a Republic Pictures actress at home.

A 1944 studio photo

publicizes Dale's role in

Lights of Old Santa Fe.

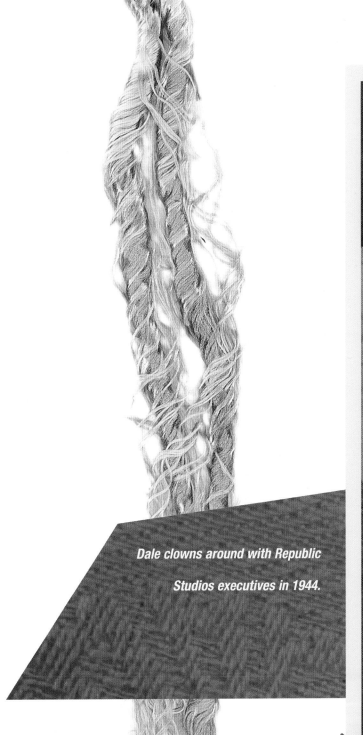

Dale clowns around with Republic
Studios executives in 1944.

Roy Rogers ropes a feisty
Dale Evans in this publicity
photo for Republic Studios.

Chapter Seven

Box-Office Star

"In real life, he stood taller than an icon and reached farther than the stars."

Country and western singer/songwriter Clint Black about Roy Rogers

Roy lent his services to the USO, entertaining troops and raising hundreds of thousands of dollars for war bonds.

Roy signs autographs for fans in 1940.

On July 12, 1943, Roy Rogers and his trusty palomino, Trigger, appeared on the cover of *Life* magazine. The overwhelming success of Roy's movies had made him the biggest box-office draw in the country.

On average, Roy made eight pictures a year, and in between productions he traveled around the country promoting his work. He sometimes made six appearances a day at various theaters where his movies were playing. Audiences would fill the seats of the movie houses, Roy and the Sons of the Pioneers would sing a few songs, and then his film would run.

Trigger accompanied Roy on all his promotional trips. Roy had acquired Trigger in 1938 when the horse was a yearling and, with the aid of a professional trainer, he brought the animal into prominence.

Along with information about his home life, the origin of the singing cowboy's name was revealed in the *Life* article. Studio executives had given Leonard Slye, also known as Dick Weston (a name Leonard picked himself and used as his professional name for a short time), the handle of Rogers in 1937, after the famous humorist Will Rogers, and Roy, which means "king." The two stage names fit together perfectly.

ROY ROGERS KING OF THE COWBOYS and TRIGGER THE SMARTEST HORSE IN THE MOVIES

The Yellow Rose of Texas

featuring DALE EVANS
with
GRANT WITHERS
HARRY SHANNON
GEORGE CLEVELAND
and
BOB NOLAN AND THE SONS OF THE PIONEERS

JOSEPH KANE — DIRECTOR

Original Screenplay by
JACK TOWNLEY

A REPUBLIC PICTURE

Roy and Dale teamed up for the second time in the 1944 movie The Yellow Rose of Texas.

Roy, Dale, and Gabby Hayes outwit the bad guys in the 1945 motion picture Bells of Rosarita.

Roy and Trigger visit a child in the hospital in 1940.

Roy plays to the camera as he boards a train in 1940 to get to his next show.

Roy rides his

palomino, Trigger.

Chapter Eight

Broadway Bound

> "I never thought of myself doing westerns. I liked cowboy pictures, but my goals were grander."
>
> *Dale Evans*—Yesterdayland Magazine, 1999

Dale, in a candid moment in 1944, with dreams of being on Broadway.

Roy and Arline Rogers admire their new daughter,

Linda Lou, born April 19, 1943.

B y the early 1940s Roy Rogers's career was at its zenith. Theater owners, echoing the sentiments of ticket buyers, named the singing cowboy the most successful Western star in America. With the help of agent Art Rush, Roy and Trigger were earning a substantial amount of money and were a highly sought-after act for rodeos and special events.

Roy's personal life was thriving as well. In 1942 Arline and Roy adopted a baby from an orphanage in Texas. Cheryl Darlene was a happy one-year-old with big eyes, and Roy knew the minute he saw her that she would be his daughter. In 1943 Arline gave birth to their second child, Linda Lou.

Conversely, Dale Evans's personal life continued to be tumultuous. Her marriage to Robert Butts ended in divorce under the strain of a busy, two-career household. Dale and her son were alone again.

Dale's career in B-rated westerns flourished, just as Roy's did, but Dale was growing increasingly worried that she would be stereotyped. She enjoyed working with Roy but could not see their partnership as long-term. Her ambition was still to star in a big, sophisticated musical.

Roy and Dale on the set of one of their movies with the Sons of the Pioneers backing them up musically.

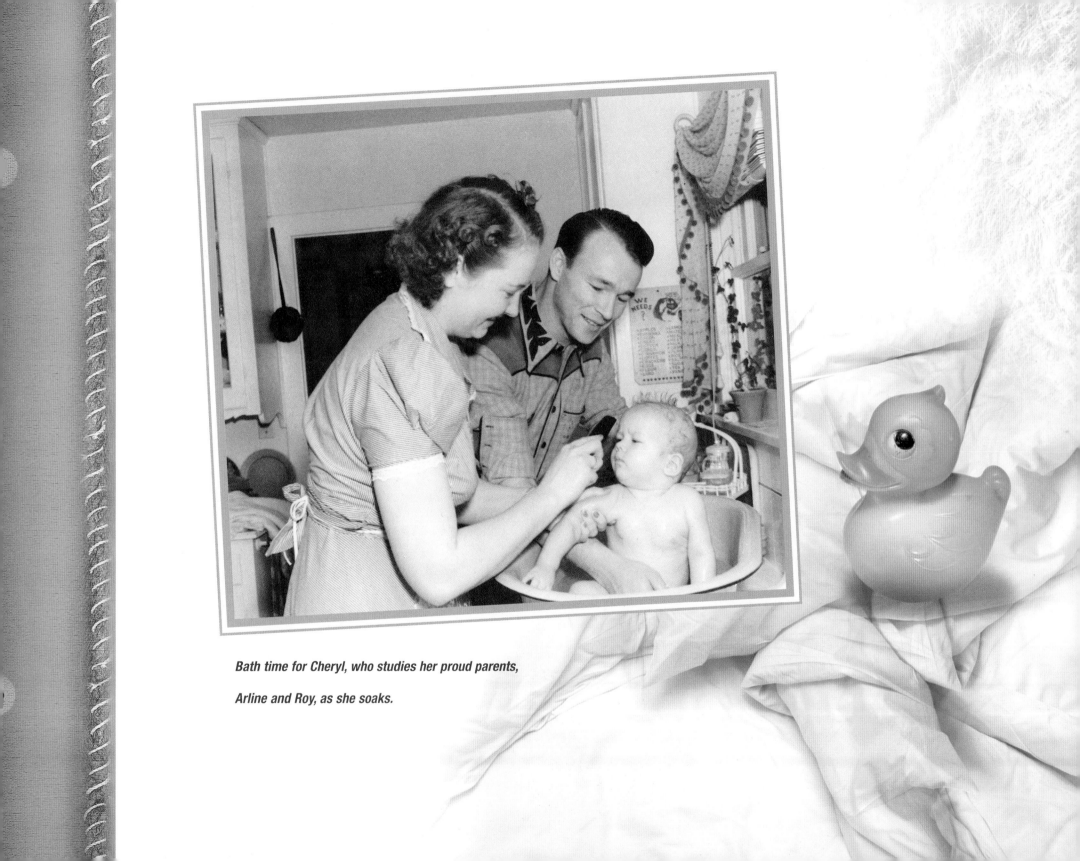

Bath time for Cheryl, who studies her proud parents,

Arline and Roy, as she soaks.

Roy, at home, carries his girls, Linda Lou

(left) and Cheryl to their room.

Roy and Dale, clowning around in 1945 on the set of Don't Fence Me In.

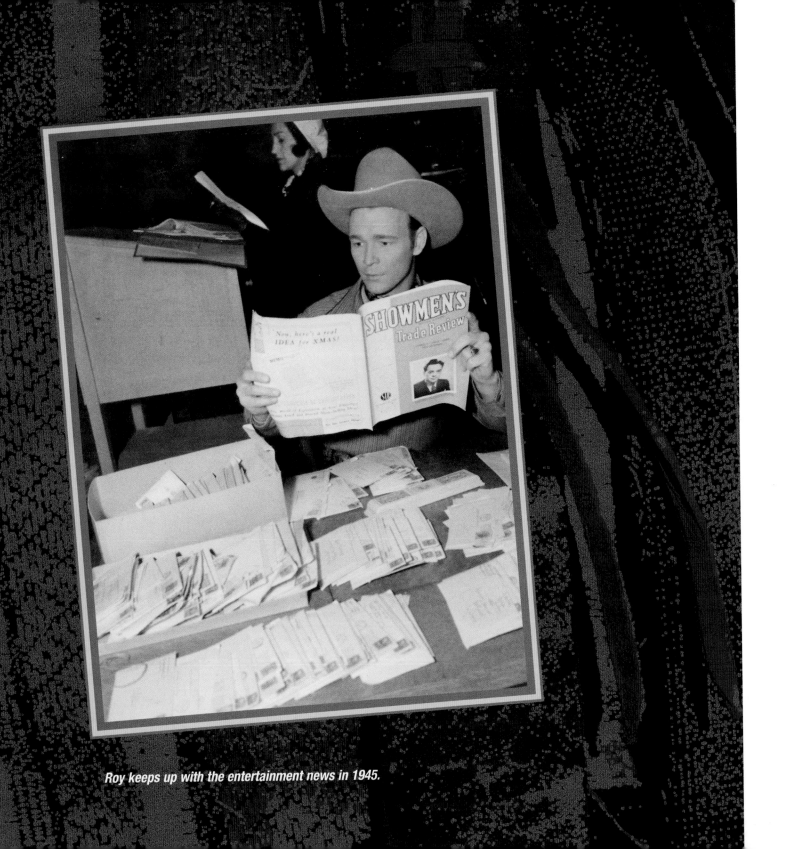

Roy keeps up with the entertainment news in 1945.

Roy surveys a chart outlining his various business ventures, which consisted of a rodeo, commercial endorsements, and even a clothing line.

Roy prepares a bottle for

daughter Linda Lou.

Chapter Nine

Monarch on Horseback

"In my judgment, based on my experience in writing about great cowboys of the past, Roy Rogers will fill the throne longer and reign over a greater public than any monarch on horseback since William S. Hart. His giving nature is all-encompassing and draws people to him."

Photoplay *reporter Jack Natteford—1946*

Trigger and Roy perform for a group of excited children, a labor of love Roy continued throughout his career.

Roy never kissed a girl in the movies, but occasionally he got a kiss from his horse.

Roy and his manager, Art Rush, look over a few of the King of the Cowboys' fan letters.

Early in Roy's career as a western star, Republic Pictures created a fictitious promotional campaign to introduce him to the public. Press agents decided it would add to Roy's appeal if they told potential moviegoers that he was a real cowboy born in Cody, Wyoming. Citizens in Wyoming and Ohio wrote to the studio protesting the false reports. Within a few days an accurate biography of Rogers was released.

The studio sent Roy on press junkets after each of his films was released. According to Republic executives, Roy came across much better in person than on the screen. They felt his eyes were more expressive and his shy smile more appealing. Fans agreed, and his personal-appearance tours proved to be profitable ventures.

Roy was grateful for his success and went out of his way to show his gratitude to his family and friends. With a portion of the money he earned, he purchased his parents a home in California and got the Sons of the Pioneers a contract working with him in all his westerns. He felt a deep sense of satisfaction to be doing something for those he loved and those who had befriended him in the lean years.

Roy practices for a radio

broadcast of Manhattan Cowboy.

Roy with the Sons of the Pioneers in 1946.

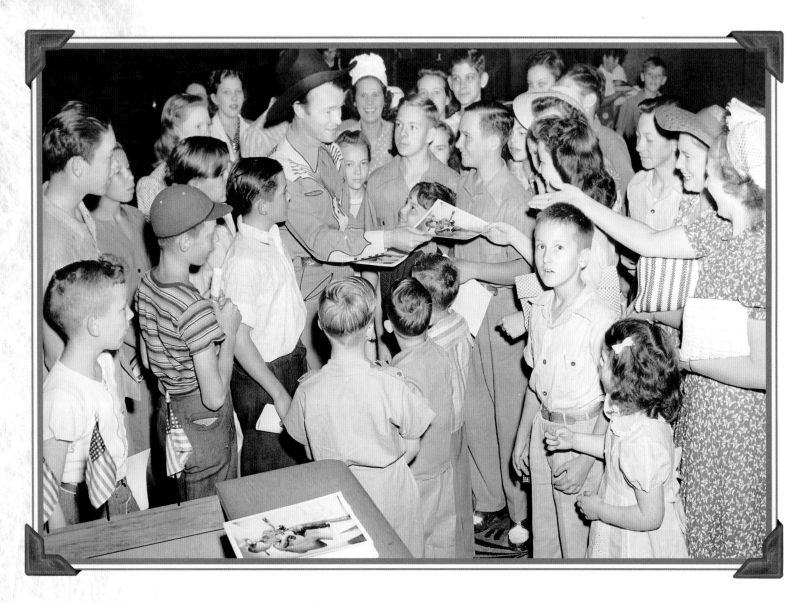

Roy Rogers never refused a young fan an autograph.

During his career Roy autographed thousands of photos.

Roy Rogers

Roy entertains onlookers with a collection of his racing pigeons.

Chapter Ten

Gabby Hayes

"He was like my father, my buddy, and my brother all wrapped up in one.
I can't say enough about him."

Roy Rogers about Gabby Hayes—Los Angeles Examiner, *1972*

Roy, Dale, and Gabby pose for a publicity photo for the

1945 movie Don't Fence Me In.

Gabby Hayes costarred with Roy and Dale in a number of films. Off screen, the accomplished stage actor spoke eloquently, wore beautiful tweed suits, and smoked a pipe.

George Hayes, better known as Gabby Hayes, began working with Roy Rogers in 1939. Before serving as sidekick to the King of the Cowboys, he made twenty-nine westerns with such stars as John Wayne and Gary Cooper. Hayes was a Shakespearean-trained actor from New York and at one time was a vaudeville performer.

Roy, and later Dale, lovingly referred to Gabby as Pappy and credited him with teaching them the craft of acting. Hayes was less like his on-stage persona than any other actor Roy and Dale worked with. He drove a Lincoln convertible, was impeccably well-groomed, and was considered by his peers to be one of the best-dressed men in Hollywood. Before the cameras began to roll he would slip into his old-timer costume, ruffle his hair, and remove his false teeth. It gave him a look that prompted producers to cast him in more than 200 westerns over his lifetime. He was one of the few motion picture sidekicks to land on the annual list of "top ten western box-office stars."

Roy and Gabby made more than forty films together between 1939 and 1946.

Chapter Eleven

A Daring Rescue

"Above all, Roy Rogers was a fine humanitarian."

Film historian Leonard Maltin—1998

Dale had limited experience on horseback when she began making westerns.

Riding lessons and tips from Roy on how to handle a bronco eventually transformed Dale into a respected horsewoman.

ale's experiences working with Roy and Gabby in their many westerns were some of the most enjoyable of her career. In one particular instance, working with them even proved to be life-saving. While the three actors and members of the crew were waiting to shoot a scene in *Helldorado,* Gabby entertained everyone with humorous stories of his vaudeville days. Dale was listening to the tale while sitting atop her horse. When the story ended she let out a loud laugh and in the process dug her heels into her ride's side. The horse took off like a shot, and Dale tried desperately to regain control of the spooked animal.

Roy quickly recognized that Dale was in trouble. Her horse was at full gallop and despite her screams, the steed would not stop. Roy quickly jumped on Trigger and took off after Dale. Once Trigger caught up to Dale, Roy reached out and scooped his costar off the frightened horse.

No one associated with a Roy Rogers movie was surprised at the actor's heroics. Roy was a great deal like the characters he played on the screen: daring, helpful, and as patient as Job.

In a letter home to her parents, Dale explained the daring rescue. She wrote that Roy was a courageous family man who talked constantly about his wife and two children. She believed that she had never met a more giving person in her life.

Both Roy and Dale loved children and made it a point

to visit their young fans no matter where they were.

Left, they pose with John Richard Mueller in 1946 at

the Catholic Youth Organization in Springfield, Illinois.

Above, Roy studies a script for another Republic western

that would team him with audience favorite Dale Evans.

HOSPITAL VISITS are always a must with Roy.

Roy gives paternalistic lecture on runaway kids

Roy Rogers and the Los Angeles Police Department didn't see eye to eye yesterday in the case of a 17-year-old Canadian youth who was picked up while hitch-hiking to Rogers' San Fernando Valley ranch.

Told by the Daily News that Martin Vok was being held in Van Nuys jail for immigration authorities, the cowboy actor cut short a busy television schedule and hurried to the police station "to straighten the kid out."

HE WAS MET with polite but firm refusal. City law, he was told, prohibited such contact with a juvenile who was in police custody.

Rogers said he only wanted to tell the boy how wrong he was. He was told the law is the law, and reminded that it's on the books for the protection of juveniles themselves.

Rogers said he was sorry he was unable to see Martin, who was taken into custody Thursday night at Chatsworth Dr. and Orion St. after telling police he

was "looking for Roy Rogers' ranch" to become a cowboy.

"NO CHILD has a right to cause his family that sort of trouble," he said. "I'm sure sorry he's in jail. I'm sorry when any kid lands in jail—but he did the wrong thing in lighting out from home and bringing grief to everyone who loves him."

Rogers said he was equally sorry the police wouldn't let him pay the fare back to St. Catherine, Ont., for the penniless youth and said he hopes other kids will "take a lesson from this."

"A kid can't go it alone like this without becoming a hobo or something worse," he said. "A youngster old enough to plan a trip like Martin made is old enough to know better."

Newspaper ads and promotional posters in cities across the world praised Roy Rogers's generosity to ailing children. Journalists often reported on the impact Roy Rogers had on American youth.

Roy and a house band perform in the 1946 film Helldorado.

Chapter Twelve

Joy and Sorrow

"He was distraught . . . Arline was his life. She managed the house, and suddenly everything was his responsibility. He hired a series of nurses, housekeepers, and companions to help with the kids, but none of them could alleviate the sense of loss he felt."

Dale Evans—The Cincinnati Enquirer, *1992*

Father and son

Dusty enjoy a

quiet moment

together.

Proud sisters Linda Lou (left) and Cheryl look in on their baby brother.

Roy and his wife, Arline, welcomed their third child into the world on October 28, 1946. They named their son Roy Rogers Jr. and gave him the nickname Dusty. A few days after their son's birth, Arline died from an embolism. The King of the Cowboys was suddenly a grieving widower with three small children to care for.

Family and friends, including Dale, came to Roy's aid, helping him prepare formula for the baby and feed and dress the girls. Roy sought comfort for his loss in his work and volunteer activities. Always interested in helping children, he began a personal campaign to cheer up sick and handicapped youngsters.

Widower Roy Rogers enjoys a moment with his children, Cheryl, Dusty, and Linda Lou (left to right).

Chapter Thirteen

Mutual Admiration

"I could never see why, if a guy is going to like a girl in the picture, why they can't have them doing something, instead of standing around with a grin and looking pretty, you know? When Dale came along . . . she gave the leading lady a better part, and the people liked it."

Roy Rogers—1978

Roy's fans brought him great comfort after his wife Arline died.

Roy and Dale charm a young fan at Madison Square Garden in 1946.

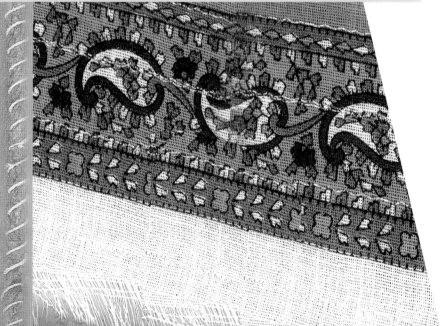

Throughout the 1940s the careers of Roy Rogers and Dale Evans rode the crest of an incredible wave. Their popularity spanned across the ocean into Europe, and fans who wanted their heroes with them at all times could purchase toothbrushes, hats, dishes, and bed sheets with the pair's names and likenesses on every item. By the late 1940s Roy Rogers and Dale Evans were second only to Walt Disney in commercial endorsements. They played to record-breaking crowds at rodeos and state fairs.

Roy and Dale were together most of their waking hours. They were good friends who confided in each other and discussed the difficulties of being single parents. They depended on one another and respected each other's talents. Roy was impressed with Dale's on-screen take-charge personality. Dale had a quick, smart-aleck delivery, and she wasn't afraid to get into a fight or two.

Roy's and Dale's mutual admiration for and attraction to one another grew. It seemed a foregone conclusion that these two western icons would ride off into the sunset together in real life.

"When I was a little girl I used to say when I grew up I was going to marry Tom Mix and I was going to have six children," Dale told *Yesterdayland* magazine in 1999. But Fate would have a different plan in store for Dale.

Below, Roy and Dale appear at the Chicago Rodeo in 1946. Right, Dale visits Roy and his family in 1946.

Chapter Fourteen

The Proposal

"Mama Dale, that's the name we gave her when she joined our family. I'm sure we were a handful . . . but she had the patience to deal with our mistrust, doubt, and resentment."

Linda Lou Rogers Johnson

Roy and Dale exchange vows on December 31, 1947.

The King of Cowboys and the Queen of the West dodge rice after their New Year's Eve wedding.

In the fall of 1947 Roy proposed to Dale as he sat on Trigger. The pair was performing at a rodeo in Chicago, and moments before their big entrance Roy suggested they get married. The date set for the wedding was New Year's Eve. Gossip columnists predicted that Trigger would be the best man and that Dale would wear a red-sequined, cowgirl gown. The predictions proved to be false.

Roy and Dale's wedding was a simple affair held at a ranch in Oklahoma, which happened to be the location for the filming of the their seventeenth movie, *Home in Oklahoma*. The couple's agent, Art Rush, served as best man and his wife, Mary Jo, was the matron of honor.

After the ceremony the newlyweds moved into a two-story Spanish-style home in Hollywood Hills. Although the Rogers children loved Dale, it was an adjustment for Cheryl, age seven, and Linda Lou, age four. They missed their mother and for a brief time resented Dale for stepping into their lives. Dusty was fifteen months old and too young to be affected by the changes.

At the suggestion of her son, Tom, Dale was able to help her new family through the transition by attending church and nurturing her relationship with the Lord. Within a few months the girls' attitude toward Dale had changed. They began to pray for one another, and a sense of peace filled their home.

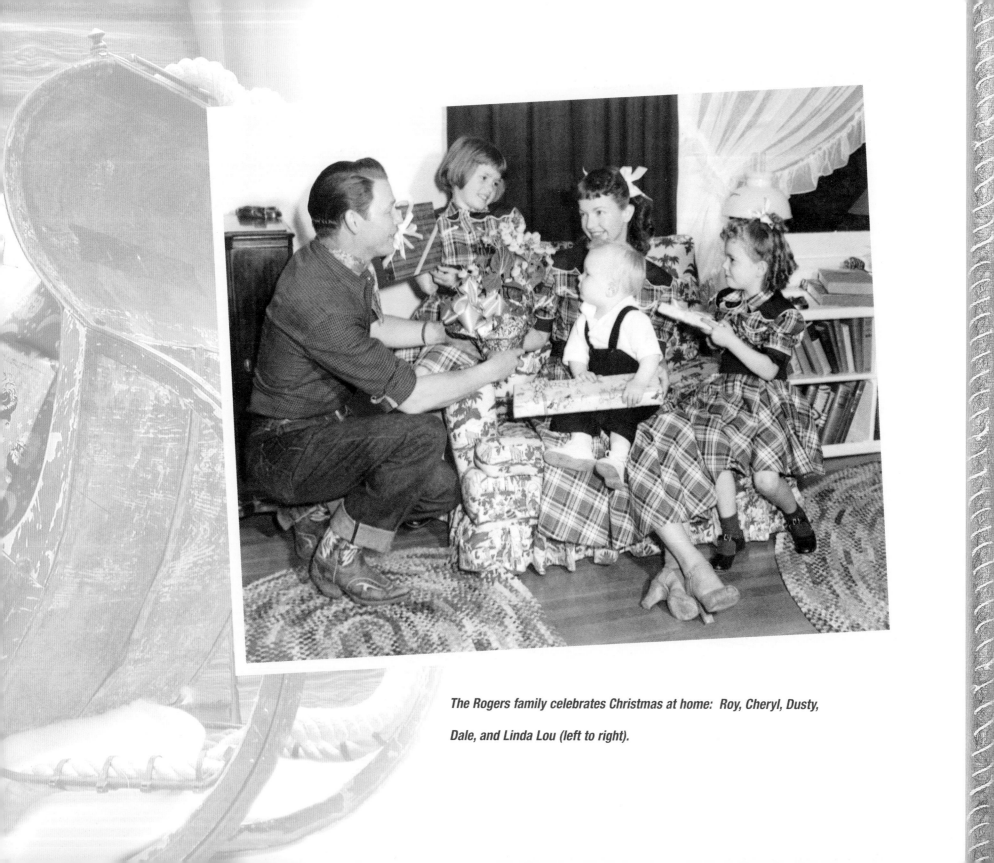

The Rogers family celebrates Christmas at home: Roy, Cheryl, Dusty,

Dale, and Linda Lou (left to right).

Dale amuses Dusty with

a toy horse in 1948.

Roy spends time with

Linda Lou and Dusty in 1948.

Chapter Fifteen

Mr. and Mrs. Roy Rogers

"He simply was a wonderful person. . . . He wasn't flashy, he was just a real person. . . .
He'd do anything for anybody. You couldn't help but love him."

Dale Evans—San Francisco Chronicle, 1996

Roy, Dale, and the Riders of the Purple Sage entertain at the Veterans Hospital in Dearborn, Michigan, on September 17, 1948.

Dale belts out a number during a radio show while Roy looks on.

Roy Rogers continued to reign as King of the Cowboys after he and Dale married, but his wife was temporarily dethroned from her honorary role as the Queen of the West. Republic Studios believed the public would not be interested in seeing a married couple teamed together, and a series of new leading ladies took Dale's place on screen. Ticket buyers did not respond well to the new women. It wasn't long before Republic executives decided to reinstate Dale and begin production on another film that would re-team the popular pair.

In between filming their westerns, Roy and Dale kept busy recording some of Dale's compositions for RCA Victor records. Their song "Aha, San Antone" sold more than 200,000 copies. Roy and Dale were also doing a radio show, performing at rodeos, and keeping up with personal-appearance tours that took them all over the United States.

Roy and Dale divided their leisure time between being with their family and entertaining veterans and children in hospitals. They noticed that many of the children in the wards were accident victims. Believing that there should be some way to reduce the child accident toll, the couple decided to team up with the National Safety Council to create a program that would call attention to this problem. They developed a plan that would give awards to elementary schools that conducted the most successful safety campaigns. Five million pupils in 11,000 elementary schools participated when the campaign got under way.

Of all the movies Dale made with Roy, her favorite was My Pal Trigger *in 1946.*

She thought it was a marvelous human-interest piece.

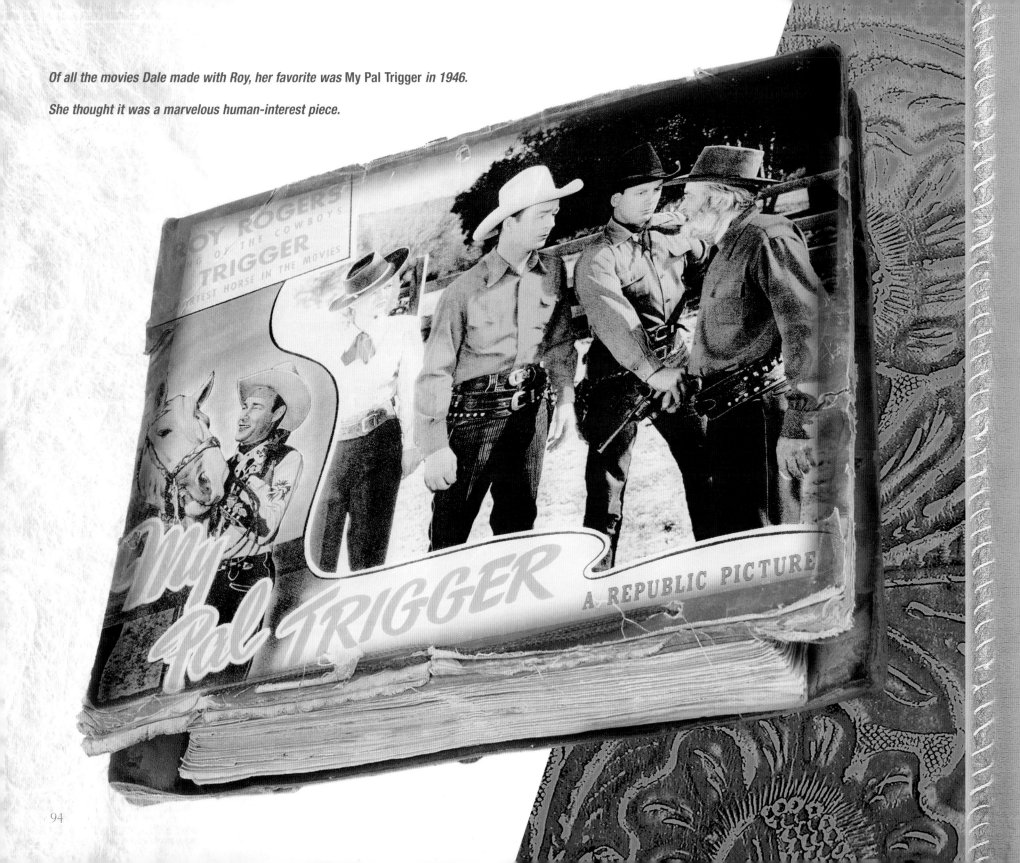

Roy and Trigger
perform for a Texas
audience in 1950.

Above, Roy, Dale, and Trigger pose for an advertisement for the Red Cross. Right, in recognition of her contributions as an entertainer for servicemen, the U.S. Navy made Dale an honorary admiral.

Chapter Sixteen

Robin Elizabeth Rogers

"No one knows exactly why these things are allowed to happen. Only God knows, and if we trust Him, some day we will understand."

Roy Rogers—Los Angeles Daily News, *1954*

Robin Elizabeth Rogers (1950–1952) was Dale and Roy's special child.

Dale and Roy enjoy feeding time with Robin.

On February 1, 1950, headlines of celebrity newspapers and magazines announced to the world that Roy and Dale were expecting a baby. The couple had been thrilled and a little shocked when they first found out they were to have a child. (After Tom was born, Dale had been told she couldn't have any other children without undergoing extensive surgery.) Thousands of fan letters congratulating them poured into the couple's headquarters in California.

Dale's pregnancy was not without complications. In addition to battling the German measles during her first trimester, she suffered with laryngitis and anemia. Dale considered the difficulties and discomfort she experienced a small price to pay for the baby she and Roy desperately wanted.

On August 26, 1950, Robin Elizabeth Rogers was born. The little girl weighed seven and a half pounds and had blonde hair and blue eyes. At his next appearance, at a rodeo in Los Angeles, Roy announced his daughter's birth to a crowd of 90,000 people. The grandstands erupted with applause over the announcement.

Robin's proud parents were making plans to take her home when their doctor told them about her health problems. The baby had been diagnosed with a defective heart and Down syndrome. Her prognosis was grave, and doctors suggested that Dale and Roy place her in an institution. The troubled couple declined that course of action and took Robin home with them.

Robin was a delicate flower and everyone in the family participated in caring for her. She was well loved and never lacked attention. The Rogers family believed God sent Robin to them to give them perspective and peace. When Roy and Dale came home after a long, hard day, they would go straight to Robin's room and scoop her up into their arms. She would smile at them, and any troubles they were having melted away.

Robin died just before her second birthday. Dale penned a book about her daughter's short life titled *Angel Unaware*. The book made best-seller lists around the country and called attention to the determination and blessings of those with Down syndrome everywhere.

Chapter Seventeen

From Tragedy to Television

"Except that his all-cowboy wardrobe is a little snappier than most, he's the type of unspoiled, unaffected, happy-go-lucky young westerner you might meet on any colorful ranch."

"From Hillbilly to Hero" in Movie Line Magazine, *1951*

Roy and Dale

sing on a Veterans

Hospital stage

in Dearborn,

Michigan, in 1948.

The Sons of the Pioneers accompany Roy and Dale at a show in Echo Park,
California, in 1952.

With the help of friends and family members, Roy and Dale were able to get through the death of their daughter and move on. They considered the live performances they did a source of great comfort. Audiences were supportive and kind. Their cheers and applause lifted Roy's and Dale's spirits and helped them through the tragedy.

The experience Roy and Dale had with Robin brought them a stronger sense of compassion for the sick and lonely children they visited in hospitals and orphanages. Their unabashed devotion to children made their personal tragedy all the more poignant. Their care and concern for all youngsters was genuine. To kids in the audience of the rodeos and movie theaters, it actually seemed that Roy and Dale worried about their safety, fun, and souls. The couple was so well loved by the public that one Hollywood gossip columinst reported that Roy could be easily elected president of the United States.

Paramount Pictures sought to take advantage of Roy's popularity. When he and Republic Studios parted ways, Paramount hired him to costar in the Bob Hope classic *Son of Paleface*.

According to a 1971 biography of Roy, he considered working with Bob Hope and female lead Jane Russell one of the most rewarding experiences of his career. He wrote a humorous article about his time on the set with Hope, titled "The Impossible Cowboy."

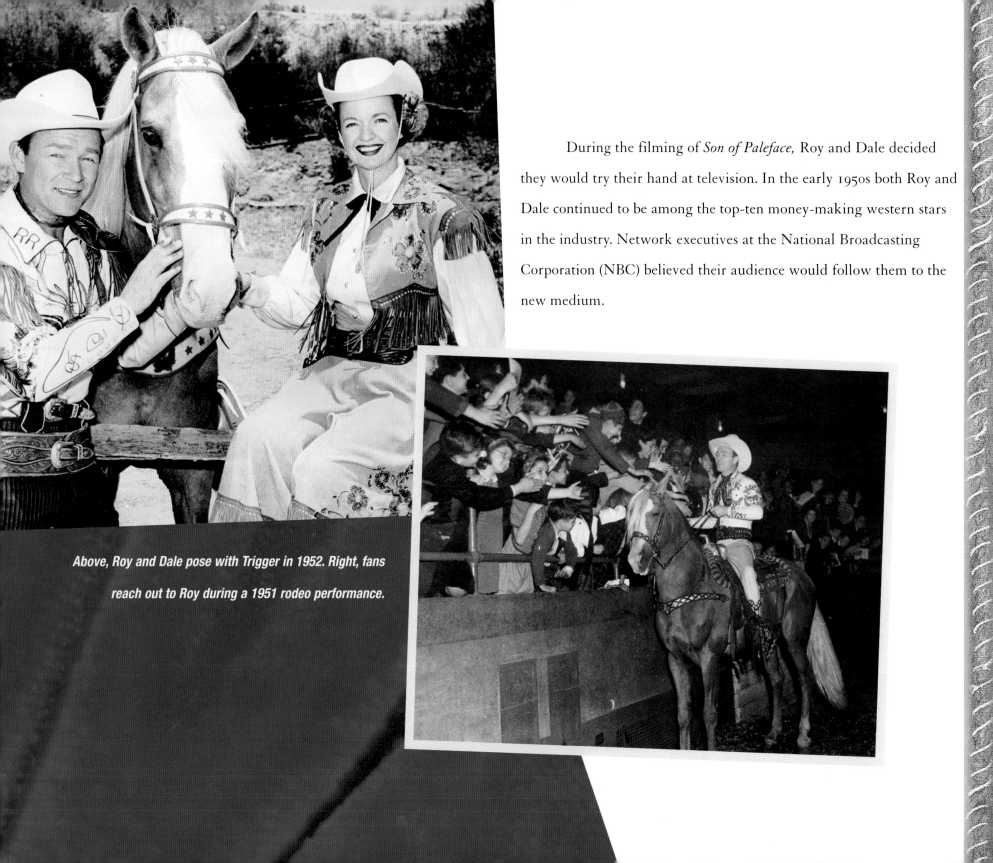

During the filming of *Son of Paleface*, Roy and Dale decided they would try their hand at television. In the early 1950s both Roy and Dale continued to be among the top-ten money-making western stars in the industry. Network executives at the National Broadcasting Corporation (NBC) believed their audience would follow them to the new medium.

Above, Roy and Dale pose with Trigger in 1952. Right, fans reach out to Roy during a 1951 rodeo performance.

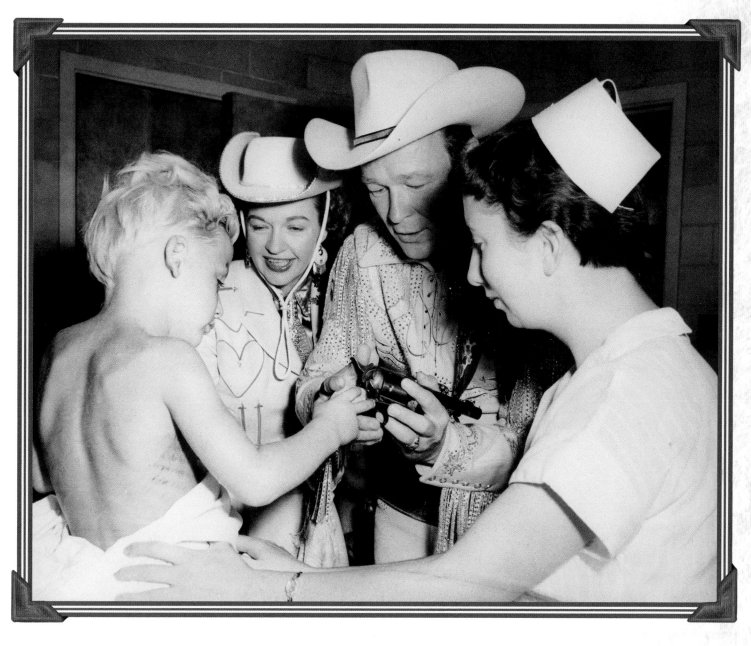

Dale and Roy make the rounds at a children's hospital in 1952.

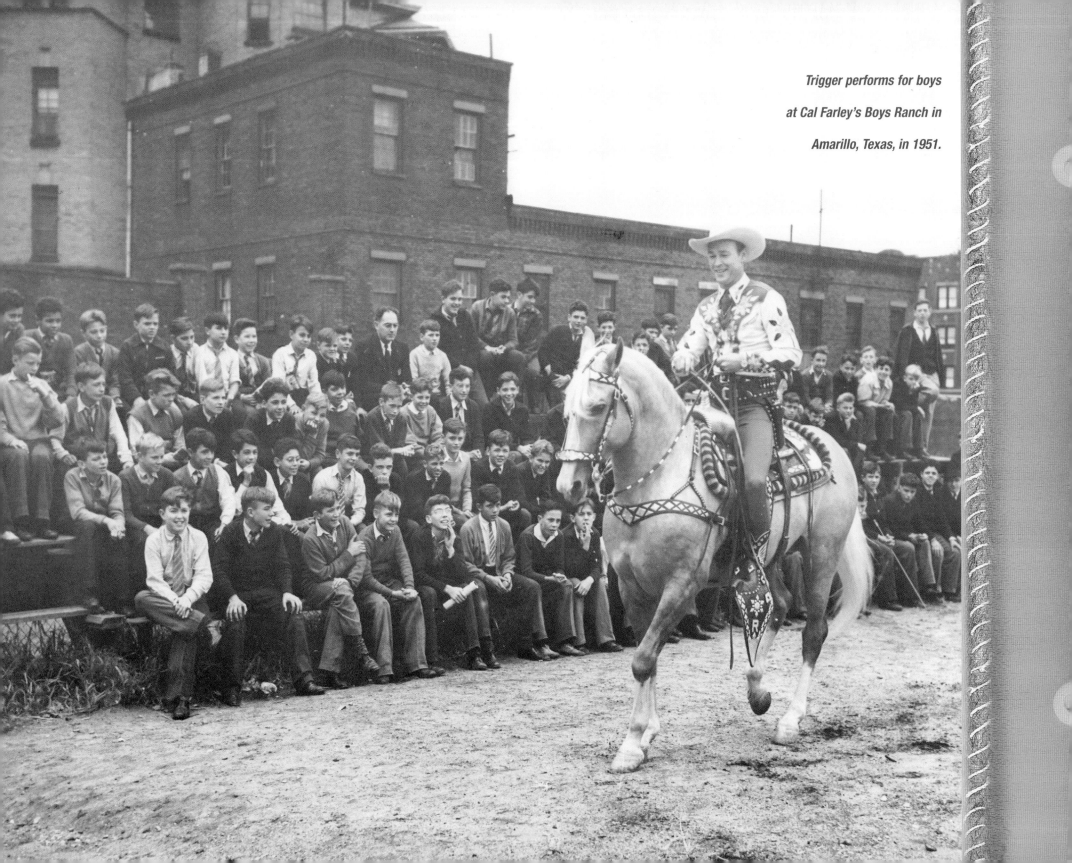

Trigger performs for boys at Cal Farley's Boys Ranch in Amarillo, Texas, in 1951.

Roy sings as he rides the range during one of his last Republic films, Grand Canyon Trail.

Roy Rogers co-starred with Bob Hope and Jane Russell

in the 1952 action comedy Son of Paleface.

HE'LL NEVER STOP THEM AT EAGLE PASS

or

BOB HOPE, THE IMPOSSIBLE COWBOY

BY ROY ROGERS

I've met up with a lot of cowboys in my time. Fast ones and slow ones, good ones and bad ones, easy-going and hot-tempered, cheerful and sad. I've known cowboys that rode like they were part of their horses, and some that rode like they hated the critters---or vice versa. I've even known cowboys that liked cows.

But never in all my born days did I ever run up against a cowboy like I just finished making a movie with.

The feller's name is Bob Hope. I don't doubt you've already heard of him; they tell me he's made quite a name for himself playing golf. The picture's name is "Son of Paleface," and I reckon you'll be seeing it soon at your nearest movie palace. That's if you want to stay on good terms with Trigger and me. (Better play safe, and see it several times.)

Now I wouldn't be setting myself up to criticize Bob Hope as a cowboy if I didn't figure this is one subject I know something about. I've been making Westerns for nigh onto fourteen years, and before that I got in some practice working as a cowhand on a ranch in New Mexico. One way and another, I've learned to know a cowboy when I see one. If Bob Hope fills the bill, then Custer stood too long, and those covered wagons should have headed East.

When all this started, Trigger and I didn't have any idea what we were letting ourselves in for. In fact, we got real excited when they told us we were to pack up our gear and mosey over to Paramount for a picture with Bob Hope. I shined up my guns and polished my boots and curried Trigger till he shone like a brand new penny. Both of us felt a little cocky when we went loping down

Marathon Street and through the Paramount Studio gate. We figured our new Western co-star would have to be pretty sharp to out-shine us.

It turned out we were the ones who needed blinders. The strong, silent half of the Hope-Crosby duo was done up in a checkered ice-cream suit, a white Panama hat, a red turtleneck sweater with a great big H on the front of it, and a floppy white linen duster. Not to mention an enormous pipe with a stem that curved like a mountain trail. He didn't need to talk---his clothes were screaming out loud.

Trigger was all for turning right around and heading home for the ranch. He's never had any truck with dudes, and he wasn't aiming to start in with this feller. Only way I could coax him back on the lot was to show him the part of the script where he gets to bite off a piece of a rainpipe Bob's climbing down, and leave Bob stranded in mid-air.

That was only the beginning. Trigger and I tried our best to make an honest cowboy out of Bob. I gave him guitar lessons, showed him how to draw from the hip, and mapped out some of the basic blows in fist-fighting. Trigger was all set to give him some riding lessons, but felt duty-bound to renege when Bob showed up for the first one with a pillow to put on the saddle.

Where all the rules of the movie range were concerned, Bob was just bound and determined to be a maverick. It sure pains me to have to read him out of the club, because Bob has a lot of nice qualities, but I'm afraid he'll never be a cowboy.

For one thing, as anybody knows, a cowboy has to be a fast man with a gun. He has to shoot straight, and he has to be able to twirl the gun like a top and then shoot straight without even taking aim. Well, sir, we never even got Bob through the twirling stage. When he started to spin the gun, his hand started to spin right with it. Had to get a locksmith to untangle his braided fingers.

It's another ironclad rule of the range that a cowboy fears nothing and

All through the picture Bob was afraid of Indians---even wooden ones---afraid of the horses, afraid of the villains. He was afraid of everyone but Jane Russell.

And that brings up another point. A cowboy's first love is his horse. Of all the rules he follows, that's Number One. Not Hope. He kept insisting he liked girls better than horses, and when I tried to show him how wrong he was, he just laughed at me.

Even with all this, there might still have been a chance for him. You can make a lot of allowances for a guy who's trying. But he went so far overboard on the regulations concerning women and horses that I'm afraid he'll find himself barred from every self-respecting corral in the country.

You probably aren't going to believe me when I tell you this, and it's a hard thing to say, but Bob Hope tried to alienate Trigger's affections. Now if there's anything that's sacred it's the love between a cowboy and his horse, and nobody'd dare try to come between the two of them. Nobody but Bob Hope.

He put on my clothes, imitated my voice, and tried to make Trigger think he was me. Even told Trigger not to listen when I called to him. Much as I dislike violence and bloodshed, I'd have had to challenge him on that one except that Trigger took care of it for me. Nobody fools Trigger; he spotted the ruse right away, and took off with Bob lickety-split until he had him hollering for mercy. If I don't miss my guess, it'll be a long time before Mr. Hope lifts his voice again to another man's horse.

But even that wasn't the crowning blow. That came when Bob, making like a cowboy and pretending to portray a true son of the old West, tried to kiss Jane Russell. Yes, he did. He not only didn't fight against making the scene; he acted as if he was going to enjoy it! Well, you know and I know that there's no such thing as love-stuff in the Westerns. A kissing scene would crack the lens of any camera trained in the ways of the Westerns.

That did it for Bob. He may go a long way in other fields---in fact, I think the lad shows lots of promise---but as a cowboy, he's plumb impossible!

###

Chapter Eighteen

The Roy Rogers Show

"His shows crammed a movie's worth of action into a half hour, and it was executed by the most accomplished actor the public had ever seen."

Max Lasswell—TV Guide, 1979

The Roy Rogers Show was not only seen on television, but it was

also heard via the radio airwaves from 1952 to 1954.

Dale warns off desperados on The Roy Rogers Show *in 1953.*

On December 30, 1951, *The Roy Rogers Show* debuted on NBC. Children across the country were poised in front of their parents' television sets on Sunday nights at 6:30 to watch their favorite singing cowboy fight for law and order in the contemporary West. The theme song for the program, written by Dale Evans, was "Happy Trails."

Dale joined Roy in the series, as did actor-singer Pat Brady, who played a bumbling sidekick. In addition to the human actors, the show featured Roy's horse, Trigger; Dale's horse, Buttermilk; her dog, Bullet; and Pat's cantankerous jeep, Nellybelle.

Critics believed the show was popular not only because audiences loved the mix of action and comedy, but also because of the high morals it brought to light. Roy and Dale's faith in God and their desire to live according to His ways were evident in each episode. (Roy read the Cowboy's Prayer at the Riders Club meetings at theaters that featured his movies and television show.) The programs struck a positive chord with children and parents alike. The show remained on the air for seven years.

Evangelist Billy Graham invited Roy and Dale to perform at his crusades and give their testimony. New attendance records were established wherever they appeared. Dale went on to record her testimony in a series of books about her life and faith. Each one was a popular seller for the publishing house, the Revell Company.

A publicity still for The Roy Rogers Show *featured this threesome in 1952.*

Although Roy and Dale gave much of themselves to their profession, the bulk of their time was focused on family. In 1954 the couple welcomed more children into their home. While on tour in Dallas, the pair decided to adopt a Choctaw baby girl and a five-year-old boy.

When Roy and Dale introduced Mary Little Doe (Dodie) and John David (Sandy) to Cheryl, Linda Lou, and Dusty, the girls showered the baby with hugs and kisses. Dusty was a bit apprehensive at first about having a brother, but he and Sandy soon became the best of friends.

The children occasionally appeared on *The Roy Rogers Show* and in commercials for the program's sponsors. The money they earned performing with their parents was set aside to be used for their education or a major purchase later in their lives.

In addition to praising God for His blessings and enjoying their growing family, Roy and Dale celebrated the high ratings their show continually received. The western movie icons had successfully made the switch from motion pictures to television.

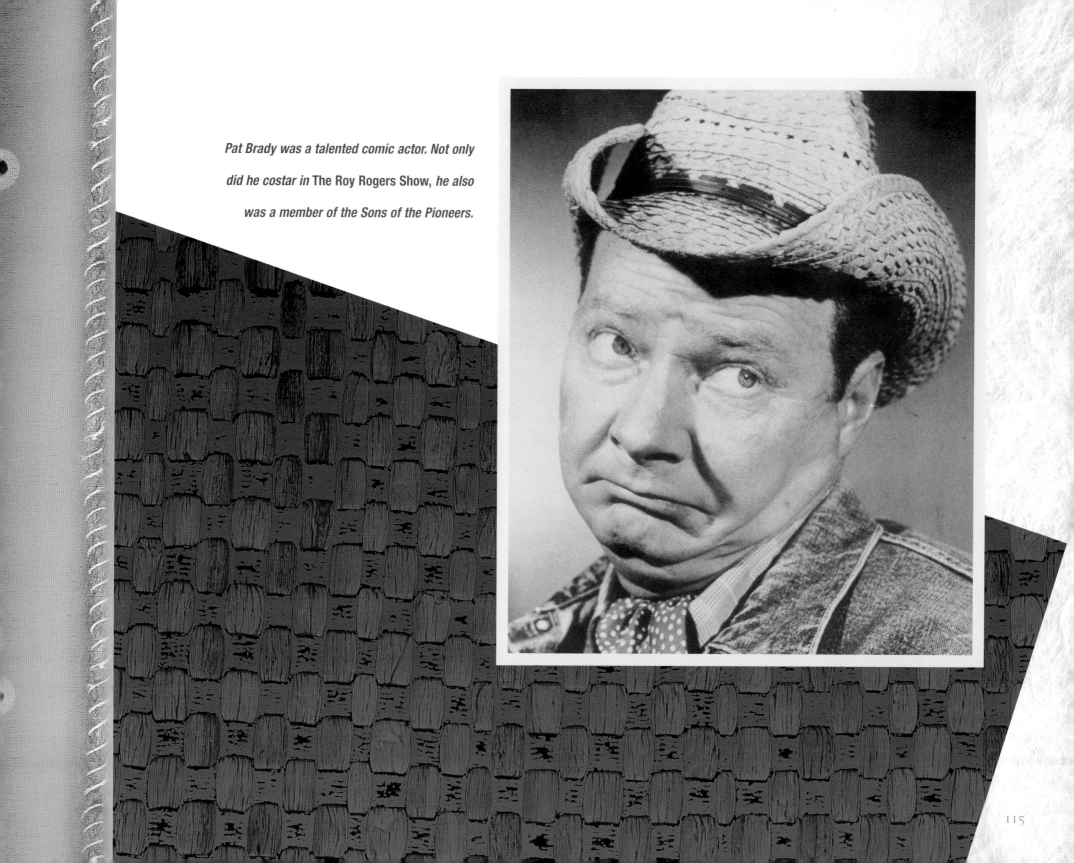

Pat Brady was a talented comic actor. Not only did he costar in The Roy Rogers Show, he also was a member of the Sons of the Pioneers.

Dale relaxes with Bullet the Wonder Dog in 1953.

Dale's follow-up book to her best seller Angel Unaware *was about her journey into faith called* My Spiritual Diary.

Bullet sits for a photo op with Roy in 1953.

Chapter Nineteen

Adding to the Family

"When they were young, they lived a life that was very fast-paced and time-consuming. Their days were long and filled with hard work. I know it wasn't easy for them to balance a family and a career, but they put a lot of time and effort into it."

Linda Lou Rogers Johnson

Dale reads to Dodie and Debbie.

Sandy, Cheryl, Dodie, Dale, Roy, Linda Lou, and Dusty (left to right)
soon made a family of seven.

Without hesitating, Roy Rogers and Dale Evans readily confessed to their fans that the best part of their lives was their family. From the beginning of Roy and Dale's relationship, children were a vital part of their household. They had always been working parents who spent time out of the limelight with their little ones, playing, helping them with homework, sharing meals, shopping for school clothes, and planning family outings. Roy and Dale loved being with their own children, and young fans everywhere dreamed of having the King of the Cowboys and the Queen of the West for a father and mother. For one young orphan girl who hoped for such parents, that dream came true when she was asked to sing for them.

In 1954 Roy and Dale traveled to Great Britain to do a few shows and appear with evangelist Billy Graham at a London crusade. When they returned to the United States, they brought another child to add to their family. She was an eleven-year-old Scottish girl named Marion Fleming. She captured their hearts when she serenaded the couple with a song about an orphaned child living on the streets.

The following year Roy and Dale adopted another girl, a three-year-old Korean War orphan whose birth name was Ai Lee. The couple renamed her Deborah Lee (Debbie). Roy and Dale had nine children and cherished every moment God allowed them to have with them.

"They spent a lot of time on the road, which caused them to miss some birthdays and special events in our lives, but they loved us, and did the best they could to provide for our needs," daughter Linda Lou recalls. "We spent quality time together, whenever possible, camping, boating, traveling, and even making snow ice cream. We lived in a fish bowl most of the time, with people taking pictures for magazines and doing interviews for television or radio. Mom and Dad were recognized wherever they went and they would always draw a crown of fans and well-wishers. We never sat down to a meal in a restaurant without an interruption by the public, but this was their life, and they were grateful for the fans who made their careers possible."

Roy, Dusty, and Sandy enjoy a bite to eat after a day fishing at Big Bear Lake.

Sandy, Roy, and Dusty are on their way to start the morning chores around the family homestead.

Dale and Roy visit a children's hospital in 1955.

Roy and Dale

rehearse for

a musical

performance

in 1953.

Sitting for a family portrait are, clockwise from left, Roy, Linda Lou, Marion, Cheryl, Dale, Dodie, Debbie, Sandy, and Dusty.

Chapter Twenty

Christmas with the Rogers Family

"When I was little, it was a family tradition to go to the Christmas tree lot and pick out a tree. We all picked our favorite tree, but Dad's choice prevailed, and we always ended up with a tree that was too tall for the ceiling in the living room. He insisted that it was going to fit, but he always ended up whittling it down two sizes."

Linda Lou Rogers Johnson

Dodie, Sandy, and a friend join Roy in Nellybelle on the set of The Roy Rogers Show.

Pictured here are (front, left to right) Roy, Dodie, Dale, and Sandy; and (back, left to right) Cheryl, Linda Lou, and Dusty.

eal time in the Rogers household was a scene of wholesome confusion. There were children talking over one another, food fights, pinching, teasing, laughing—normal behavior at any family table. It was a hectic home life, one that Roy and Dale relished. Their son Dusty later said that it was only when he got older and looked back on his life that he recognized how unique and special his family was. As a boy it had all seemed quite normal. His parents were western film icons, but to the Rogers children they were simply Mom and Dad.

"They played with us and took us on vacation, and spanked us when we needed it," Dusty recalled in 2002. "Dad went to work like other dads, but his work was in the field of entertainment. I never thought of my mother as anything but Mom, and although working mothers were unusual when I was a kid, I can't remember thinking of my mom's work as being anything special."

Some of the most important times for Roy and Dale at home were the holidays: Christmas, Easter, Thanksgiving, Fourth of July. "They loved the holiday season because they were family times," remembers daughter Linda Lou.

"When we got the tree home, we spent the evening drinking hot chocolate with marshmallows, making apple Santa Clauses, and decorating the tree," Linda Lou recalls. "Dad would string the lights and put the tree topper in place, while Mom helped us string popcorn and cranberries into garlands and hang our favorite ornament on the tree. When our task was completed, we had the lighting ceremony. Dad stood back with a smile on his face and the joy of seeing a job well done.

"On Christmas morning, we all attended the service at our Church to celebrate the true meaning of Christmas, which is the birth of our Lord and Savior Jesus Christ, and to give Him thanks for all of our many blessings. Then we returned home to open our presents."

Columnist Louella Parsons wrote about the Rogers family Christmas in 1954.

The Roy Rogers Plan a Merry Christmas Roundup

By LOUELLA O. PARSONS
Motion Picture Editor
International News Service

IN THE big Dale Evans-Roy Rogers ranch house in Encino there will be an old-fashioned Christmas this year. Their six children—four adopted and Roy's own two—will gather around the Christmas tree which they will string with popcorn and cranberries and bright, shiny ornaments.

The happiest one in the group will be 13-year-old Marion Fleming, the Scotch orphan Dale and Roy brought back from Europe after they heard her sing "Who Will Buy My Flowers?" in such a wistful tone that Roy told me he almost burst out crying.

Dale said, "We try to visit the hospitals and orphanages when we're on tour. This child we just couldn't leave behind. She was undernourished and had had three homes. She's gained 18 pounds since we've had her. Marion's best Christmas present came when we received a cable from Chief Constable William Merrilees in Edinburgh giving us permission to keep her with us and educate her. She is very talented and has already taught Linda Lou to dance."

"When I told her she could stay," Roy interrupted, "she threw her arms around my neck and said, 'This is the happiest day of my life, and all my wishes have come true!'"

But Marion is only one of the happy children who will gather

LOUELLA O. PARSONS *Exclusive!*

Conrad Mercurio

DALE EVANS (standing at left) aids Linda Lou as Roy and Dusty look on. Seated are Dodie, Marion, Sandy. Cheryl was in school.

(Read Louella O. Parsons every day in the Examiner)

around that Christmas tree. In the Encino home, a-swarm with youngsters, is Sandy, 7, whom they adopted when he was a very sick child and who is perfectly healthy now; Doe, or Dodie as they call her, who is a 2½-year-old Choctaw Indian girl; Cheryl, 14 and a beauty, who is in school at Kemper Hall in Kenosha, Wis.; Dusty, or Roy Rogers Jr., 8, and Linda Lou, 11. Dusty and Linda are Roy's own children by a former marriage. Their mother died when Dusty was born, and he has never known any mother but Dale.

At luncheon, we had a chance to talk. I asked Dale how she manages with all those different temperaments.

"Oh, it's easy," she replied. "We have no problem with the adopted children. I just tell them I am adopted, too; that God is our Father

and He chose Roy and me to bring them into our home. I ask the children whose real parents are living to pray for them because I feel they must need spiritual help to have given up their children."

After the death of their little daughter, Robin Elizabeth, both Dale and Roy became deeply religious.

She pulled a picture of little Doe out of her purse (both Dale and Roy carry pictures of all the children) and said, "Dodie filled a big void in our lives after Robin died. You know Roy has Choctaw Indian blood, so little Doe is very proud to say she is 'just like Daddy.' She is very talented; she sings, rides a horse and can outrun anyone I've ever seen."

To house this many takes a lot of room, but the Rogers have taken care of this. Their house has five

bedrooms and there are four guest houses on the ranch.

"We have a watchdog that sleeps in the girls' bedroom," said Roy, "and he'd tear anybody to pieces who walked through their door."

"It must be a problem to feed that crowd," I couldn't help remarking.

"Not too bad," Roy said. "We raise our own beef, lamb, chickens, turkeys, and most of our own vegetables. Recently, I brought home some pigeons, and Dusty, who has become a Cub Scout, and the eight members of his troop are busy building coops to house them. They plan to raise the birds on their own."

There are no two harder working people in Hollywood than the talented and popular Roy and his equally talented and popular wife. They spent five months on tour this

year and Dale says it's the last trip for her. She'll continue with Roy's radio show, but she doesn't expect to be on his TV shows. She's going to stay home with the children as much as possible.

"What will you do if Dale doesn't travel?" I asked Roy.

He laughed and said, "I'll tell you a secret. I'm staying home, too. Done all the traveling I want to do for a long while."

"Do your children realize you're the great Roy Rogers, or do they think of you just as their Daddy?" I asked Roy.

"Well, I can answer that with something that actually happened a few nights ago," he said. "Dusty and I were watching one of my old films on TV. Trigger and I were just about to get our man when Dusty yelled, 'Look, look, Daddy! There goes Roy Rogers now!'"

PICTORIAL LIVING

11

Chapter Twenty-One

Dearest Debbie

"It's amazing the tragedies they've survived. Lesser people would be bitter and angry with God, but they weren't. In fact, just the opposite. Roy Rogers and Dale Evans . . . I've never met such wonderful people."

Pete Plamondori—Daily Sentry News, *1976*

Roy and Dale wave goodbye to friends and family from the rocks above their home in Chatsworth, California.

Dale is surrounded by fans in 1964.

Roy and Dale's happy trails were once again interrupted by hard times in 1964 and 1965. The first tragedy occurred in 1964 during the week of Debbie's twelfth birthday. While on a goodwill trip to Tijuana, Mexico, with members of her church, the youngster was killed in a bus accident. The news of the loss of their daughter devastated the couple.

Dusty reminded a sorrowful Dale that Debbie was with the Lord and that Dale needed to trust God and depend on His strength. Roy, who was in the hospital recovering from back and neck surgery when he heard about his child, became distraught and was immediately transferred to the intensive care unit.

Once again, Roy's and Dale's spirits were lifted by the outpouring of sympathy and affection from their fans. Both found comfort in performing for those loyal followers after Roy was released from the hospital. Dale worked through the hurt by writing about her daughter and the impact she had made on all their lives. *Dearest Debbie* was a heartfelt tribute to another beloved Rogers child who had gone home. Royalties from the book went to World Vision Inc., the organization that had helped Roy and Dale find and adopt Debbie.

Left, Roy, Dale, and Trigger
visit fans at a boys' ranch.
Below, Roy spends time with a
few special friends in 1964.

Chapter Twenty-Two

PFC Sandy Rogers

"I want to serve my country. I want to prove myself a man."

Sandy Rogers—1964

Dale poses for a publicity photo.

A little more than a year after Debbie was killed, the Rogerses received news that Sandy had died. Sandy had been in the Army, stationed in Germany. He had dreamed of being a soldier for many years. As a boy, he delighted in toy soldiers, guns, and airplanes, promising that when he grew up he would drive a tank.

The road to enlistment had not been an easy one for Sandy. He had been subjected to years of abuse by his biological parents, which left him with a slight problem with his eyes, a malformed head, and weakness in his bones from malnutrition. He worked hard to eventually be strong enough to join the military, and in January 1965 he convinced Roy and Dale to let him drop out of high school and enlist.

Sandy wanted to serve in Vietnam, but Army recruiters felt that his reflexes weren't fast enough for such an assignment. After basic training in Missouri and a short tour in Tennessee, Sandy was sent to Germany to serve as a member of the tank corps.

After returning from field maneuvers with his platoon in October 1965, Sandy decided to attend a party and celebrate his promotion from private to private first class.

Responding to a dare, he drank a lot of hard liquor. His buddies poured the inebriated young man into his bunk, thinking he would

Roy captures a quiet moment before a performance.

sleep off his intoxication. But tragically, in the middle of the night, Sandy vomited and choked to death.

A distraught Roy and Dale laid their son to rest at the Forest Lawn Memorial Park Cemetery alongside their other two deceased children. The Rogers family wept as a military bugler played "Taps" and Dale was presented with the flag that had been draped over Sandy's coffin.

Just as before, Dale managed to get through the grieving process by writing. The book *Salute to Sandy* was a tribute to their courageous son and his struggle to find a place for himself in the world.

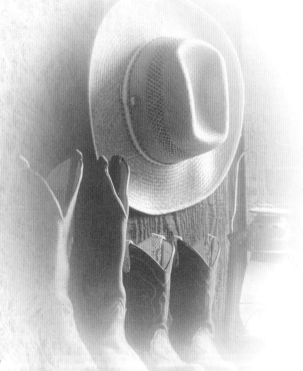

Roy with Dusty (left) and Sandy when they were young.

Chapter Twenty-Three

Touring with the USO

"I asked Momma how she could manage to go on after losing another baby. She told me it helped to know they were all together in Heaven with the Lord."

Marion Fleming Rogers

Dale and Roy entertain troops in Vietnam in 1966.

Roy and Dale participate in a Billy Graham Crusade.

When Roy Rogers and Dale Evans were asked to join the USO and entertain troops in Vietnam in 1966, they quickly agreed. Their reasons were twofold. First, they felt it would be a way of honoring their son Sandy, because he had longed to serve his country there. Second, they wanted to learn for themselves about the United States' involvement in the Asian war.

The USO tour in which the couple took part included a musical group known as the Travelon Combo and western ballad singer Wayne West. The show kicked off at the USO headquarters in Saigon. Members of the appreciative audience included enlisted men, officers, and medical staff from a nearby medical unit. From there the group entertained 327 troops at the Third Field Hospital. For two weeks Roy, Dale, and the other members of the show endured manic weather and traveled through dense jungle and brush to entertain soldiers in big halls and mud huts.

It was a moving experience for the Rogerses, one that left them immensely proud of the American troops. The soldiers' bravery and idealism in the face of great danger gave Roy and Dale strength and hope to carry on.

Halfway through the tour Dale met a young man who had been in Sandy's company in Germany. He was not one of the troops that had been with Sandy the night he died. He told Dale that if he had been present, the tragedy wouldn't have happened. He went on to assure her that her son had been a good soldier.

Before Roy and Dale left Vietnam, they were presented with citations "For Service to Morale of Armed Forces in Southeast Asia."

Dale and Roy at the Texas A&M stadium.

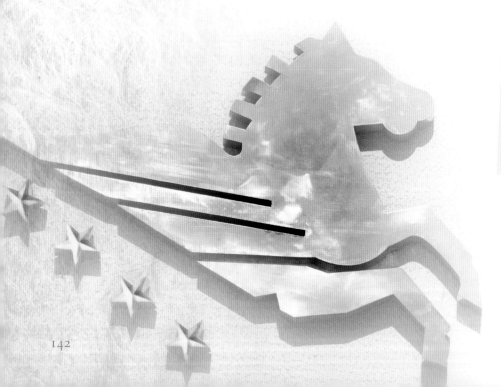

Chapter Twenty-Four

No Slowing Down

"They put on quite a spread a couple of weeks ago at the ol' Twentieth Century-Fox lot, buckaroos. It was the third annual *Fall Guy* wrap party and this year it honored the season's last guest star, Roy Rogers."

Drama-Logue *magazine, 1984*

Dale and Roy salute fans with another western star, Gene Autry.

Dale and Roy appear with Roy Clark on **Hee Haw.**

For most people, retirement is a time to withdraw from business or public life. Roy and Dale's idea of retiring was nothing of the sort. In many respects their golden years were as busy as ever. Well into their sixties, the couple continued to attend state fairs and rodeos, setting new box-office records at every venue.

Throughout the 1960s, '70s, and '80s, Roy and Dale hosted a variety of programs for the ABC network. They also appeared on *Hee-Haw,* the *Muppet Show*, Christmas specials, talk shows, and Billy Graham crusades. Dale continued to write books on the subjects of faith and family and traveled to Christian rallies all over the country, sharing her message in word and song. Roy guest-starred on the popular television series *The Fall Guy* and the made-for-television movies like *Alias Jesse James* and *The Gambler.*

Dale and Roy left lasting impressions on the cast and crew wherever they performed. On many occasions their co-workers went out of their way to express appreciation for Roy and Dale's influence on the industry.

An article in a 1984 issue of *Drama-Logue* magazine described the third annual *Fall Guy* wrap party that honored Roy.

"Yup, Stage 20 looked like the Ponderosa run amok with bales of hay, a stagecoach, country music, and grub piled high on miles of gingham-covered tables. Chicken, ribs, chili, corn bread, potato

145

Roy and Dale with Mike Douglas on **The Mike Douglas Show.**

salad and, according to one server, 'low-octane beans' were devoured by the western-attired Hollywood crowd. Mink with buckskins and tiaras with moccasins mingled and munched as Rogers and his bride of thirty-six years, Dale Evans, wandered through the festivities.

"Series executive producer Glen A. Larson greeted folks with the jest, 'My mother used to take me to see Roy Rogers and Lee Majors when I was a kid.' The object of his fun, *Fall Guy* star Lee Majors, joined Larson on stage and announced he saw Roy Rogers 'for twenty-five cents when I was a kid.'

"Obviously now feeling 300 years old, Rogers hopped youthfully on stage, looking like 33. He looked terrific in a turquoise-blue glittering cowboy suit complete with fringe. He ain't the King of Cowboys for nothing! 'I can go anyplace because I've grown up with everyone,' said the King. 'I've been trying to retire for ten years, but no one will let me!' It must be true. This is the second time around as a *Fall Guy* guest star."

Chapter Twenty-Five

The Last Picture

"I'm an introvert at heart. And show business—even though I've loved it so much—has always been hard for me."

Roy Rogers—Drama-Logue magazine, 1984

Roy and Dale make a personal appearance at a Veterans of Foreign Wars event in Victorville, California.

Dale and Roy appeared on the television program Hee Haw seven times.

Roy and Dale made time in their retirement schedule for visits with their children and grandchildren. Other activities they enjoyed were playing golf, bowling, big game hunting, and riding their motorcycle across the high desert where they lived in Apple Valley, California.

In 1976 Roy returned to the big screen in a film called *Mackintosh and T.J.* It was a modern western in which Roy played a ranch hand and drifter who took a young man into his care and helped him grow up. Critics hailed Rogers's performance and credited the strength of the film to his "presence and genial decency of intent."

PRAYER

Oh, Lord, I reckon I'n not much just by myself.

I've failed to do a lotta things I oughta do.

But Lord, when trails are steep and passes high,

Help me to ride it straight the whole way through.

And in the falling dusk when I get the final call,

I do not care how many flowers they send.

Above all else, the happiest trail would be

For you to say to me: Let's ride my friend.....Amen

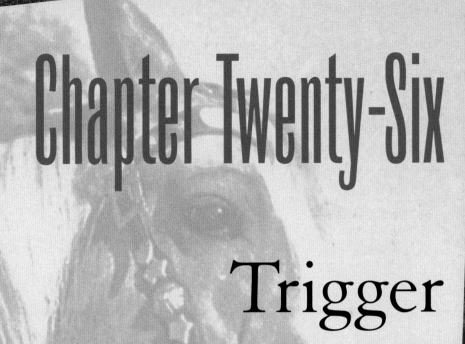

Chapter Twenty-Six

Trigger

"He was a fabulous horse. He was pretty and handled himself well. He was really something."

Roy Rogers — Drama-Logue *magazine, 1984*

Trigger shows off on the set of The Roy Rogers Show.

Trigger was billed as "the smartest horse in the movies."

There's almost nothing more important to a cowboy than his horse. He depends on his reliable steed to help him with his job and to be his friend and all-around partner through thick and thin. Throughout the 1930s, '40s, and '50s, Roy Rogers was the quintessential cowboy, but a big part of his heroic appeal was his palomino, Trigger. Billed as "the smartest horse in movies," Trigger was Roy's riding partner in eighty films and one hundred television shows.

Roy purchased Trigger in 1938 from Hudkins Stables in Los Angeles for $2,500. He knew Trigger was a special horse the moment he saw him trotting through a field. With the help of expert horse trainer Glenn Randall, Roy worked with Trigger to teach him a myriad of tricks, including counting, writing, and bowing to an audience.

Trigger's fame grew with every new Roy Rogers movie. The horse was a star with four stand-ins. He made $750 a week and received 200 fan letters a month. In 1940 Roy insured the valuable animal for $100,000.

In the mid 1940s Roy received a substantial offer from a wealthy Texan to purchase Trigger. Roy refused the $200,000 sum and promised worried fans that he "wouldn't sell Trigger for all the money in Texas."

Trigger died in July 1965, having reached the age of thirty-three. Roy grieved for a long time over the loss of his old friend. Trigger's look-alike, Trigger Junior, took the palomino's place in rodeos and state fairs.

Above, Trigger gives Dale a ride she'll never

forget in 1945. Right, Roy and Trigger pose in a

publicity photo for The Roy Rogers Show.

Chapter Twenty-Seven

The Roy Rogers— Dale Evans Museum

"Dale Evans and Roy Rogers are synonymous with wholesome and fun entertainment for the whole family. Their entire lives were dedicated to living their faith and values in movies, TV, and anywhere they could be used to enrich our country. They are sorely missed in today's deteriorating culture."

Best-selling author and minister Tim LaHaye

An estimated 200,000 people visit the Roy Rogers–Dale Evans Museum in Branson, Missouri, each year.

During the mid-1940s fans purchased two million comic books a month about the adventures of Roy Rogers and Dale Evans.

From 1976 to 1998 travelers making their way through Southern California along Route 66 could stop off at the town of Victorville and visit with the King of the Cowboys and the Queen of the West personally. The Roy Rogers–Dale Evans Museum was located on forty acres of land just off the interstate. Grownups who recalled going to Roy Rogers–Dale Evans movies or watching the two on their television show congregated at the museum to relive childhood memories. On most mornings Roy and Dale would be there signing autographs and shaking hands with faithful fans who had always held them in high esteem.

The Rogers museum is a unique gallery, containing not so much archives from the Old West as personal items from western movie icons. Patrons can wax nostalgic as they roam the halls of the building looking at Roy Rogers's pistols, parade saddles, and comic books.

From the moment Roy's career began to take off, he dreamed of having a museum. He kept mementos such as watches, boots, and spurs in hopes of one day putting the items on display.

The first museum Roy and Dale opened was in Apple Valley, California, in the late 1960s. The couple purchased a bowling alley and had it refurbished to show off their collection of fan letters, awards, and photographs, among many other keepsakes.

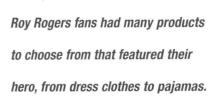

Roy Rogers fans had many products to choose from that featured their hero, from dress clothes to pajamas.

Many Happy Trails
Roy Rogers
Trigger

Roy and Trigger strike a familiar pose.

In 1976 the museum was moved to a bigger building in Victorville, California. The new facility was twice the size of the previous museum, but Roy and Dale had no problem filling the additional display areas. Besides viewing the pair's fancy rodeo clothes, hats, and gauntlets, visitors could also get a look at their dining room table, dishes, and family Bible.

Of course, the most popular exhibit was Trigger, mounted and shown rearing on his hind legs. At one time the Smithsonian Institution had asked for the palomino's remains, but Roy had decided to display his old friend closer to home.

Roy Rogers's and Dale Evans's legacies live on through their new museum in Branson, Missouri. The entire original collection is there, along with more costumes and memorabilia from the silver screen. It is estimated that more than 200,000 people visit the museum each year.

More than five decades have passed since Roy and Dale rode the celluloid range together, and they continue to be loved and admired in a way that few, if any, celebrities can claim.

Children of all ages enjoyed eating the Post products their hero Roy Rogers endorsed.

Roy Rogers Filmography

1935
Slightly Static
The Old Homestead
Way Up Thar
Gallant Defender

1936
The Mystery Avenger
Rhythm on the Range
Song of the Saddle
California Mail
The Big Show
The Old Corral

1937
The Old Wyoming Trail
Wild Horse Rodeo

1938
The Old Barn Dance
Under Western Stars
Billy the Kid Returns
Come On, Rangers
Shine On, Harvest Moon

1939
Rough Riders' Round-up
Southward Ho
Frontier Pony Express
In Old Caliente
Wall Street Cowboy

The Arizona Kid
Jeepers Creepers
Saga of Death Valley
Days of Jesse James

1940
The Dark Command
Young Buffalo Bill
The Carson City Kid

The Ranger and the Lady
Colorado
Young Bill Hickok
The Border Legion

1941
Robin Hood of the Pecos
Arkansas Judge
In Old Cheyenne

Roy and Dale pose with Trigger and Buttermilk on the set of The Roy Rogers Show.

Sheriff of Tombstone
Nevada City
Bad Man of Deadwood
Jesse James at Bay
Red River Valley

1942
Man from Cheyenne
South of Santa Fe
Sunset on the Desert
Romance on the Range
Sons of the Pioneers
Sunset Serenade
Heart of the Golden West
Ridin' Down the Canyon

1943
Idaho
King of the Cowboys
Song of Texas
Silver Spurs
Man from Music Mountain
Hands Across the Border

1944
The Cowboy and the Senorita
The Yellow Rose of Texas
Song of Nevada
San Fernando Valley
Lights of Old Santa Fe

Brazil

Lake Placid Serenade

Hollywood Canteen

1945

Utah

Where Do We Go from Here?

Bells of Rosarita

The Man from Oklahoma

Along the Navajo Trail

Sunset in El Dorado

Don't Fence Me In

1946

Song of Arizona

Rainbow over Texas

My Pal Trigger

Under Nevada Skies

Roll On Texas Moon

Home in Oklahoma

Out California Way

Helldorado

1947

Apache Rose

Bells of San Angelo

Springtime in the Sierras

On the Old Spanish Trail

1948

The Gay Ranchero

Under California Stars

Eyes of Texas

Melody Time

Night Time in Nevada

Grand Canyon Trail

The Far Frontier

The posters advertise Hands Across the Border, *1943;* Yellow Rose of Texas, *1944;*
and Song of Nevada, *1944.*

1949

Susanna Pass

Down Dakota Way

The Golden Stallion

1950

Bells of Coronado

Twilight in the Sierras

Trigger, Jr.

Sunset in the West

North of the Great Divide

Trail of Robin Hood

1951

Spoilers of the Plains

Heart of the Rockies

In Old Amarillo

South of Caliente

Pals of the Golden West

The Roy Rogers Show (TV
Series)

1952

Son of Paleface

1953

Alias Jesse James

1962–1963

The Roy Rogers and Dale Evans
Show (TV Series)

1976

Mackintosh and T.J.

1983

The Gambler: The Adventure
Continues

Dale Evans Filmography

1942
Orchestra Wives
Girl Trouble

1943
Swing Your Partner
West Side Kid
Hoosier Holiday
Here Comes Elmer
In Old Oklahoma

1944
Casanova in Burlesque
The Cowboy and the Senorita
The Yellow Rose of Texas
Song of Nevada
San Fernando Valley
Lights of Old Santa Fe

1945
The Big Show-Off
Utah
Bells of Rosarita
The Man from Oklahoma
Hitchhike to Happiness
Along the Navajo Trail
Sunset in El Dorado
Don't Fence Me In

1946
Song of Arizona
Rainbow over Texas
My Pal Trigger
Under Nevada Skies

Roll On Texas Moon
Home in Oklahoma
Out California Way
Helldorado

1947
Apache Rose
Bells of San Angelo
The Trespasser

1948
Slippy McGee

1949
Susanna Pass
Down Dakota Way
The Golden Stallion

1950
Bells of Coronado
Twilight in the Sierras
Trigger, Jr.

1951
South of Caliente
Pals of the Golden West
The Roy Rogers Show (TV Series)

1962–1963
The Roy Rogers and Dale Evans
   Show (TV Series)

1976
Mackintosh and T.J.

Cowboy Roy Rogers swings his senorita, Dale Evans, in a Republic Studios publicity photo.

This 1944 poster publicized The Yellow Rose of Texas.

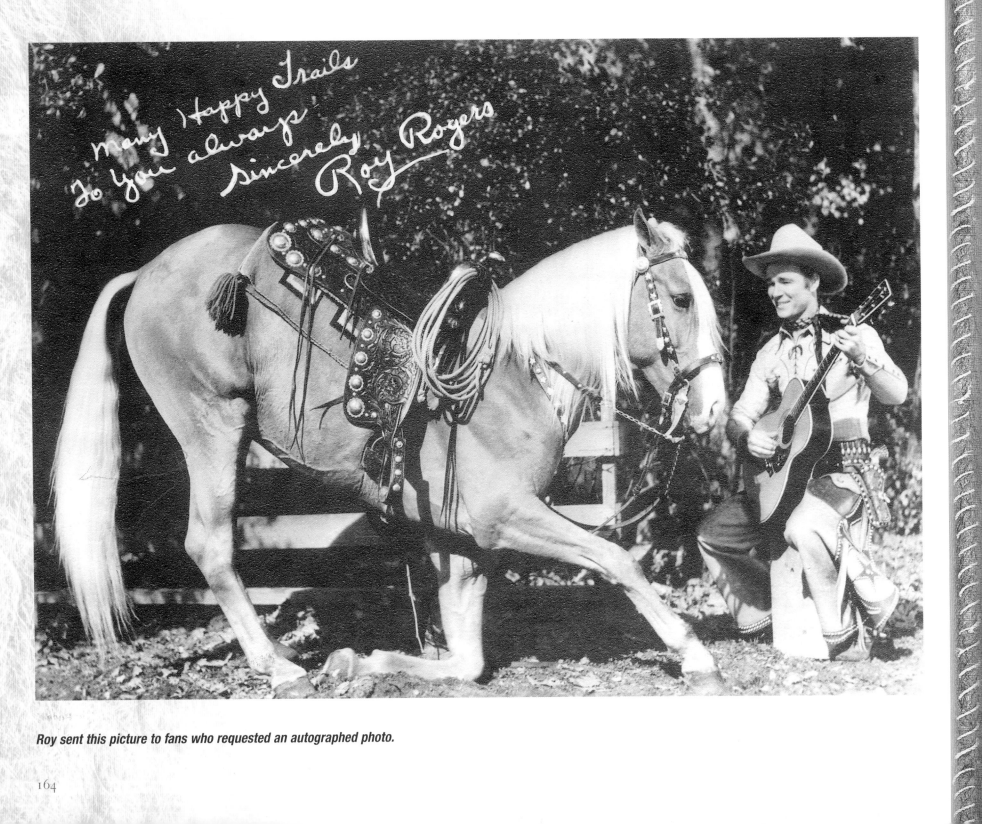

Many Happy Trails To You always Sincerely Roy Rogers

Roy sent this picture to fans who requested an autographed photo.

Bibliography

Books

Hardy, Phil. *The Western Film Encyclopedia.* Overlook Press, Woodstock, New York, 1983.

Rogers, Dale Evans. *Angel Unaware.* Fleming H. Revell Company, Westwood, New Jersey, 1953.

———. *My Spiritual Diary.* Fleming H. Revell Company, Old Tappan, New Jersey, 1955.

———. *To My Son: Faith at Our House.* Fleming H. Revell Company, Westwood, New Jersey, 1957.

———. *Dearest Debbie.* Fleming H. Revell Company, Westwood, New Jersey, 1965.

———. *Salute to Sandy.* Fleming H. Revell Company, Westwood, New Jersey, 1967.

———. *The Woman at the Well.* Fleming H. Revell Company, Old Tappan, New Jersey, 1970.

———. *Dale: My Personal Picture Album.* Fleming H. Revell Company, Old Tappan, New Jersey, 1971.

Rogers, Dale Evans, and Norman Rohrer. *Rainbow on a Hard Trail.* Fleming H. Revell, Grand Rapids, Michigan, 1999.

Rogers, Roy, Dale Evans, and Carlton Stowers. *Happy Trails.* Word Books, Waco, Texas, 1979.

Rogers, Roy Jr., and Karen A. Wojahn. *Growing Up With Roy & Dale.* Regal Books, Ventura, California, 1986.

Roper, William L. *Roy Rogers: King of the Cowboys.* T. S. Denison & Company, Inc., Minneapolis, Minnesota, 1971.

Stern, Michael, and Jane Stern. *Happy Trails: Our Life Story.* Simon & Schuster, New York, New York, 1994.

Newspapers and Periodicals

"Come Visit Roy Rogers," *Radio and Mirror 32,* No. 32 (August, 1949).

Billboard, October 9, 1954.

The Cincinnati Enquirer, September 30, 2002.

Cowboys and Indians Magazine, Archives, 2001.

The Daily Sentry News, September 12, 1976.

Dallas Daily Press, July 7 and 8, 1998.

Dallas Morning Journal, Sunday Magazine, March 11, 1984.

Drama-Logue, March 15, 1984.

H Magazine, August 1998.

The Hollywood Reporter, May 19, 1954.

Life Magazine, July 12, 1943.

Look Magazine, January 16, 1951.

Los Angeles Daily News, August 7, 1954.

Los Angeles Examiner, December 26, 1950.

Los Angeles Times, May 2003.

Modern Screen, November 1941.

Movie Line Magazine, April 1944.

New York Times Magazine, November 4, 1945.

Photoplay Magazine, November 11, 1941.

Portsmouth Times, Portsmouth, Ohio, August 1959.

Press Dispatch, July 12, 1998.

Sacramento Bee, December 12, 1959.

Saturday Evening Post, June 9, 1945.

TV Guide 3, No. 114 (June 4, 1955).

Variety Magazine, April 6, 1966.

Yesterdayland Magazine, 1999.

Interviews

Fleming, Marion, October 6, 2003, Grass Valley, California.

Fox, Thomas, January 14, 2004, Sacramento, California.

Rogers, Roy Jr., September 14, 2002, Victorville, California.

To Chris Enss from Linda Johnson, October 6, 2003.

Roy Rogers and Dale Evans wave to fans at one of the hundreds of parades they appeared in during their long career.

Index

About the Authors

Howard Kazanjian is an award-winning producer and entertainment executive who has been producing feature films and television programs for more than twenty-five years. While vice president of production for Lucasfilm Ltd., he produced two of the highest-grossing films of all time: *Raiders of the Lost Ark* and *Star Wars: Return of the Jedi.* He also managed production of another top-ten box-office hit, *The Empire Strikes Back.* Some of his other notable credits include *The Rookies, Demolition Man,* and the two-hour pilot and first season of *J.A.G.*

In addition to his production experience, Kazanjian has worked with some of the finest directors in the history of cinema. He has worked closely with such legends as Alfred Hitchcock, Billy Wilder, Sam Peckinpah, Robert Wise, Joshua Logan, Clint Eastwood, George Lucas, Steven Spielberg, and Francis Ford Coppola. He is a longtime voting member of the Academy of Motion Picture Arts and Sciences, the Academy of Television Arts and Sciences, the Producers Guild of America, and the Directors Guild of America. The California native is also a trustee of Azusa Pacific University.

Chris Enss is an author, scriptwriter, and comedienne who has written for television and film and performed on cruise ships and on stage. She co-wrote and voiced one-minute vignettes on gold rush history for KNCO radio in Grass Valley, California, and produced an audiotape about the Yuba Donner Scenic Byway for the Tahoe National Forest, which led to her first book, *With Great Hope: Women of the California Gold Rush.* Her other books include *Love Untamed: Romances of the Old West, Gilded Girls: Women Entertainers of the Old West, She Wore a Yellow Ribbon: Women Soldiers and Patriots of the Western Frontier,* and *The Cowboy and the Senorita: A Biography of Roy Rogers and Dale Evans,* co-authored with Howard Kazanjian.